HEART OF DARKNESS
&
THE SECRET SHARER

NOTES

including
- *Life of the Author*
- *Introductions to the Novels*
- *Lists of Characters*
- *Brief Plot Synopses*
- *Summaries & Critical Commentaries*
- *Critical Essays*
- *Suggested Essay Topics*
- *Selected Bibliography*

by
Norma Youngbirg

INCORPORATED

LINCOLN, NEBRASKA 68501

Editor	Consulting Editor
Gary Carey, M.A.	*James L. Roberts, Ph.D.*
University of Colorado	*Department of English*
	University of Nebraska

ISBN 0-8220-0587-5
© Copyright 1988, 1965
by
Cliffs Notes, Inc.
All Rights Reserved
Printed in U.S.A.

1999 Printing

Cliffs Notes, Inc.   Lincoln, Nebraska

CONTENTS

Heart of Darkness

The Secret Sharer

Summaries and Commentaries

Critical Essays

Suggested Essay Topics

Selected Bibliography

HEART OF DARKNESS
Notes

LIFE OF THE AUTHOR

Joseph Conrad was born Teodor Jozef Konrad Korzeniowski on December 3, 1857, the only child of a patriotic Polish couple living in the southern Polish Ukraine. Conrad's father was esteemed as a translator of Shakespeare, as well as a poet and a man of letters in Poland, and Conrad's mother was a gentle, well-born lady with a keen mind but frail health.

When Conrad was five, his father was arrested for allegedly taking part in revolutionary plots against the Russians and was exiled to northern Russia; Conrad and his mother went with him. His mother died from the hardships of prison life three years later; she was only thirty-four.

Conrad's father sent him back to his mother's brother for his education, and Conrad was never to see him again. The poet-patriot lived only four more years. Conrad was eleven years old, but the emotional bond between him and his father was so strong that a deep melancholy settled within the young boy; much of his writing as an adult is marked by a melancholy undercurrent.

Conrad received a good education in Cracow, Poland, and after a trip through Italy and Switzerland, he decided not to return to his father's homeland. Poland held no promise; already Conrad had suffered too much from the country's Russian landlords. Instead, the young lad decided on a career very different from what one might expect of a boy brought up in Poland; he chose the sea as his vocation.

Conrad reached Marseilles in October of 1874, when he was seventeen, and for the next twenty years, he sailed almost continually. Not surprisingly, most of his novels and short stories have the sea as a background for the action and as a symbolic parallel for their heroes' inner turbulence. In fact, most of Conrad's work concerns the sea. There is very little old-fashioned romantic interest in his novels.

Part of this romantic void may be due to the fact that while Conrad was in Marseilles and only seventeen, he had his first love affair. It ended in disaster. For some time, Conrad told people that he had been wounded in a duel, but now it seems clear that he tried to commit suicide.

Conrad left Marseilles in April of 1878, when he was twenty-one, and it was then that he first saw England. He knew no English, but he signed on an English ship making voyages between Lowestoft and Newcastle. It was on that ship that he began to learn English.

At twenty-four, Conrad was made first mate of a ship that touched down in Singapore, and it was here that he learned about an incident that would later become the kernel of the plot for *Lord Jim*. Then, four years later, while Conrad was aboard the *Vidar*, he met Jim Lingard, the sailor who would become the physical model for Lord Jim; in fact, all the men aboard the *Vidar* called Jim "Lord Jim."

In 1886, when Conrad was twenty-nine, he became a British subject, and the same year, he wrote his first short story, "The Black Mate." He submitted it to a literary competition, but was unsuccessful. This failure, however, did not stop him from continuing to write. During the next three years, in order to fill empty, boring hours while he was at sea, Conrad began his first novel, *Almayer's Folly*. In addition, he continued writing diaries and journals when he transferred onto a Congo River steamer the following year, making notes that would eventually become the basis for one of his masterpieces, *Heart of Darkness*.

Conrad's health was weakened in Africa, and so he returned to England to recover his strength. Then in 1894, when Conrad was thirty-seven, he returned to sea; he also completed *Almayer's Folly*. The novel appeared the following year, and Conrad left the sea. He married Jessie George, a woman seventeen years his junior. She was a woman with no literary or intellectual interests, but Conrad continued to write with intense, careful seriousness. *Heart of Darkness* was first serialized in *Blackwood's Magazine*; it appeared soon afterward as a single volume, and Conrad then turned his time to *Lord Jim*, his twelfth work of fiction.

After only a cursory reading of *Lord Jim*, it is almost impossible to believe that its author did not learn English until he was twenty-one. The novel has a philosophical depth that is profound and a vocabulary that is rich and exact. In addition, the structure of the novel is masterfully inventive; clearly, Conrad was attempting a leap forward in the genre of the novel as he constructed his novel with multiple narratives, striking symbolism, time shifts, and multi-layer characterizations.

After *Lord Jim*, Conrad produced one major novel after another – *Nostromo, Typhoon, The Secret Agent, Under Western Eyes, Victory*, and *Chance*, perhaps his most "popular" novel. He was no longer poor, and, ironically, he was no longer superlatively productive. From 1911 until his death in 1924, he never wrote anything that equaled his early works. His great work was done.

Personally, however, Conrad's life was full. He was recognized widely, and he enjoyed dressing the part of a dandy; it was something he had always enjoyed doing, and now he could financially afford to. He played this role with great enthusiasm. He was a short, tiny man and had a sharp Slavic face which he accentuated with a short beard, and he was playing the "aristocrat," as it were. No one minded, for within literary circles, Conrad was exactly that – a master.

When World War I broke out, Conrad was spending some time in Poland with his wife and sons, and they barely escaped imprisonment. Back in England, Conrad began assembling his entire body of work, which appeared in 1920, and immediately afterward, he was offered a knighthood by the British government. He declined, however, and continued living without national honor, but with immense literary honor instead. He suffered a heart attack in August, 1924, and was buried at Canterbury.

LIST OF CHARACTERS

Marlow

Charlie Marlow is thirty-two years old and has always followed the sea. His voyage up the Congo River, however, is his first experience in freshwater navigation. Conrad uses Marlow as a narrator so that he himself can enter the story and tell it out of his own philosophical mind.

The sight of wasted human life and ruined supplies shocks Marlow. The manager's senseless cruelty and gross folly overwhelm him with anger and disgust. He longs to see Kurtz – a fabulously successful ivory agent and the target of the company manager's spite. More and more, Marlow turns from the white people (because of their ruthless brutality) and to the dark jungle (a symbol of reality and truth), and, finally, he comes to fully appreciate black people. In addition, he identifies more and more with Kurtz—long before he even sees the man and talks to him. In the end, the affinity between the two men becomes a symbolic unity. Marlow and Kurtz are the light and dark selves of a single person. Marlow is what Kurtz might have been, and Kurtz is what Marlow might have become.

Kurtz

Like Marlow, Kurtz comes to the Congo with noble intentions. He thinks that each ivory station should stand like a beacon light, offering a better way of life to the natives. Kurtz has a half-English mother and a half-French father. He has been educated partly in England and speaks English. The culture and civilization of Europe have contributed to the making of Kurtz; he is an orator, writer, poet, musician, artist, politician, ivory procurer, and chief agent of the ivory company's Inner Station at Stanley Falls. In short, he is a "universal genius"; he is also a "hollow man," a man without basic integrity or any sense of social responsibility.

At the end of his descent into the lowest pit of degradation, Kurtz is also a thief, murderer, raider, persecutor, and to climax all of his other shady practices, he allows himself to be worshipped as a god. Marlow does not see Kurtz, however, until Kurtz is so emaciated by disease that he looks more like a ruined piece of a man than a whole human being. There is no trace of Kurtz' former good looks nor his former good health. Marlow remarks that Kurtz' head is as bald as an ivory ball and that he resembles "an animated image of death carved out of old ivory."

Kurtz wins control of men through fear and adoration. His power over the natives almost destroys Marlow and the party aboard the steamboat. Kurtz is the lusty, violent devil whom Marlow describes at the story's beginning. He is contrasted with the manager, who is weak and flabby—the weak and flabby devil also described by Marlow. Kurtz is a victim of the manager's murderous cruelty; stronger men than Kurtz would have found virtuous behavior difficult under the manager's criminal neglect. It is possible that Kurtz might never have revealed his evil nature if he had not been cornered and tortured by the manager.

The Manager

This character, based upon a real person, Camille Delcommune, is the ultimate villain of the plot. He is directly or indirectly to blame for all the disorder, waste, cruelty, and neglect that curses all three stations. He is in charge of all. Marlow suggests that the manager arranged to wreck Marlow's steamboat in order to delay sending help to Kurtz. He also deliberately prevents rivets from coming up from the coast to complete the steamboat's repairs.

At the manager's command, a native black boy is beaten unmercifully for a fire which burns up a shed full of "trash." (The boy is probably innocent.) The manager's conversation with his uncle reveals the full, treacherous nature of both men. His physical appearance is ordinary; his talents are few. Excellent health gives him an advantage over other men. He seems to "have no entrails" and has been in the Congo for nine years. His blue eyes look remarkably cold, and his look can fall on a man "like an axe-blow."

The Brickmaker

Despite his title, he is a man who seemingly makes no bricks; instead, he acts as the manager's secretary, and he is responsible for a good deal of the plot's entangling elements. For example:

- He reveals the reason why the manager hates Marlow.
- He shows Marlow the painting which Kurtz left at the Central Station (one of the important symbols of the book).
- He reveals the reason why the manager hates Kurtz.
- He unwillingly and indirectly lets Marlow know that the delay in getting rivets is intentional.
- He lets Marlow know that the white men at the Central Station identify Marlow with Kurtz, as members of the "new gang of virtue."

The Russian

He typifies the kind of person who, with "sheer fright and fine sentiments," always manages to be safe — regardless of the circumstances. He gives Marlow an insight into the terrible nature of Kurtz' surrender to the wilderness.

The Immaculate Accountant

He is the keeper of all the company books; he gives Marlow the first information about Kurtz, and he also reveals the general hatred which the white men bear toward the blacks. In addition, he confides his conviction that there is shady business at the Central Station.

Kurtz' Intended

She presents much of the "white truth" about Kurtz to Marlow.

The Foreman (the Boilermaker)

He is a humble worker, despised by the pilgrims, but he is one of Marlow's few friends; he shows us that Marlow does have friends, and Marlow likes him especially because he works. Marlow has great respect for work.

The Uncle of the Manager

He seems almost as depraved as his nephew, the manager. He makes no secret of their murderous intent toward Kurtz. His conversation with the manager supplies the information that Kurtz started down the river with a load of ivory nine months ago, traveling three hundred miles, then turned back and retraced his voyage in a single dugout with native rowers.

The Fireman

He typifies the sort of civilization and enlightenment which the ivory company provides for the natives.

The Helmsman

Because of the helmsman's violent death, Marlow is awakened to a deep kinship with black people. The helmsman's death also alerts Marlow to the starving condition of the cannibal crew.

Kurtz' Black Mistress

She is a contrast to the white girl who waits for Kurtz in Europe.

The Knitting Women

In the Brussels office, they sit and knit and portend the dark experience which is awaiting Marlow in Africa.

The Swedish Captain

He takes Marlow to the company's Outer Station and gives Marlow the first intimation that the colonization efforts in Africa are far from altruistic; from him, Marlow learns that life in the Belgian Congo can be deadly dangerous.

The Pilgrims

They are the human counterparts of the huge, buzzing, "stabbing" flies that hover over the dying agent in the accountant's immaculate office. They are ivory-hungry vultures, opportunists who fawn upon the manager and hope for some lucky break that will make them rich. Marlow calls them "pilgrims" because they always carry staffs (Matthew 10:10).

The Black People

In a climactic moment in the novel, Marlow recognizes that although he is a cultured, civilized European white man, he is a "brother" to the so-called savage blacks. In this novel, note that, in general, the "white" souls belong to the black men and that the "black" souls belong to the white men.

The Dying Agent

Tormented by the stabbing flies in the accountant's office, he symbolizes the inhuman treatment accorded the men who come under the general manager's care.

BRIEF PLOT SYNOPSIS

Heart of Darkness is really two stories—(1) the story of Charlie Marlow's trip from the civilization of Europe to the primitive interior of an uncivilized continent (Africa) and back home again (Conrad *does not* name the Congo River or the Belgian Congo region of Africa, nor does he identify Africa itself, but he infers by details of travel and geography that the river which carries Marlow's steamer to Kurtz' station is indeed the Congo, and that the continent is Africa. However, Conrad *does* identify the Thames River and Europe – the river and continent of the civilized, known world.); and (2) it is also the story of the conflict between the manager of an ivory company and Kurtz, an ivory agent. The interplay of these two stories constitutes the plot of *Heart of Darkness,* and it is the effect of Story No. 2 on Story No. 1 which carries the theme, or unifying principle, of the novel.

At the beginning of *Heart of Darkness,* the yawl (sailboat) *Nellie* lies at anchor in the Thames, awaiting the turn of the tide. On her deck, five persons sit watching the great stir of lights in the river: they are the owner of the boat, a lawyer, an accountant, the narrator (who does not identify himself as to profession), and Marlow, the only one present who still follows the sea.

To this group of listeners, Marlow spins a tale of his only experience with fresh water sailing. He prefaces the story by a reference to ancient times in Britain when "This, too, [was once] one of the dark places of the earth."

Home from his seafaring in the Far East, he tired of his long vacation and tried to find another ship. Through the influence of an aunt, he secured a job with a company engaged in the ivory trade. Marlow found that everyone in the company office treated him like a doomed person; he found out why later.

He left Europe on a French steamer. From the time he boarded the ship, his whole adventure took on an unreal dream quality, as though he were voyaging into the regions of fantasy. The languid sea, the monotonous coastline, and his isolation seemed to keep him "away from the truth of things." The black men who came out to trade with the ship fascinated and delighted him. They were of real substance, brief contacts with reality.

Marlow left the French ship at the river's mouth and took passage on a river boat commanded by a Swede. The captain's remarks about the government and the country troubled Marlow. The captain related how he took a Swedish compatriot up the river, and the fellow hanged himself. When Marlow asked why, the captain said, "The sun too much for him, or the country perhaps."

After a hundred-mile trip, Marlow landed at the company's Outer Station, and the waste he saw everywhere appalled him. Valuable machinery, tools, and materials lay about in the grass, rusting and broken. A gang of chained black men clanked past him. He turned from the blinding sunlight into a grove of trees and found that it sheltered a throng of dying black workers, animated skeletons, worn out and sickened through labor for the company.

Marlow hurried up the slope to the company buildings and met an astonishing creature – a vision in a high-starched collar, huge white cuffs and elegant clothes. This "fashion model" proved to be the company's chief accountant, the man who kept the books for the ivory operation. He had been there three years, and his quarters were as neat as his clothing. Everything else about the station was chaotic.

From this man, Marlow first heard of Kurtz. The accountant described Kurtz as a first-class agent, a remarkable person in charge of an important station. He sent down more ivory than all the other agents combined. The accountant also confided that Kurtz was in line for a big promotion. He would be *somebody* in administration before long.

After ten hot and disappointing days at the Outer Station, Marlow set out with a caravan of sixty blacks and one white man for the two-hundred-mile trek overland to the company's Central Station. Each of his carriers had a sixty-pound load strapped to his back. The white man proved a poor traveler and had to be carried, thus causing trouble with the carriers. The man was much too heavy.

The trek took fifteen days, and Marlow hobbled into the Central Station only to discover that his steamboat was at the bottom of the river. His informant said that it would be "all right"; the manager himself was there and waiting to see him now.

The manager was far from courteous. Although he knew that Marlow had just come two hundred miles over a difficult trail, the manager did not ask him to sit down. He began babbling at once about the wreck. He didn't know whether Mr. Kurtz was alive or dead. He estimated that it would take three months to raise the steamer and repair it.

Marlow decided that the manager was a "chattering idiot" and turned his back on him and the station. He gave his full attention to raising the sunken steamboat. He could not, however, avoid observing the "pilgrims" – a group of sixteen to twenty white men who carried long staffs and loitered around the station talking about ivory in reverential tones.

One evening a shed full of cheap trade goods caught fire and burned down. Marlow went to look and overheard the manager discussing Kurtz with one of the agents, a hook-nosed fellow with eyes like mica.

Later, the brickmaker invited Marlow to his room. Marlow marveled at the elegance of the young agent's quarters – compared with the rest of the station. Marlow thought that the agent must be in favor with the manager, and he realized that the agent wanted to pump him, trying to find out about Marlow's influential friends back in Belgium. Marlow did not reveal anything. He let the man believe what he wanted to.

On his way out the door, Marlow saw a small sketch in oils on a panel. It pictured a draped and blindfolded woman carrying a lighted torch. The agent explained that Kurtz painted the picture at the Central Station more than a year ago.

Marlow questioned him further about Kurtz. He discovered that the agent expected Kurtz to be promoted within a year. He said that Marlow surely must know what else the company had planned for Kurtz because Marlow and Kurtz both belonged to the "new gang of virtue" and were recommended by the same sources in Europe. Marlow could hardly suppress a laugh. He asked the agent if he read the company's private correspondence. The man didn't reply, and Marlow assured him that when Kurtz became general manager, he would not have the opportunity to do so any more.

The agent snuffed the candle and they went outside, where the "papier mâché Mephistopheles," as Marlow calls him, rambled on, still trying to extract some information. Clearly, this agent wanted to be assistant manager of the Central Station; naturally, he resented Kurtz. Strangely, Marlow realized, the agent had been sent out to make bricks, but he had been at the station for over a year and had made no bricks. He did only secretarial work for the manager.

Marlow told the agent that he needed rivets to repair the steamer. For weeks, he had been trying to get rivets without success. He knew that black carriers came every week bringing supplies from the lower station, but they were always loaded with cheap trade goods – never with rivets. Marlow reminded the agent that he, the manager's secretary, should be able to get the rivets. The agent said that he ordered only what he was dictated to order. Marlow demanded action on the rivets, but the agent turned cool and changed the subject. Many more weeks passed before any rivets showed up.

After the agent left, Marlow went aboard his steamer and found another white man—a boilermaker by trade and a fine workman, although the pilgrims despised him. Marlow told him that they were going to get rivets, and together they danced triumphantly on the steamer's deck.

Instead of rivets, however, an "invasion" arrived, an invasion by the Eldorado Expedition, whose leader was the manager's uncle. Marlow overheard enough of their conversation to understand the manager's attitude toward Kurtz. In over a year, the manager had made no effort to provide supplies for the Inner Station. Kurtz started down the river some months ago, but after descending three hundred miles with his shipment of ivory, he decided to turn back, leaving his half-caste clerk to complete the delivery. The clerk reported that Kurtz had been very ill and had not fully recovered. Now, no news had come from Kurtz for nine months.

At last, rivets arrived and Marlow repaired the steamboat and set out on a voyage upriver with the manager and three or four pilgrims onboard. A crew of twenty natives kept the engine boiler going and ran the steamer. The journey took two months; the steamer seemed to crawl. To Marlow, however, it crawled toward one object—Kurtz. In the jungle along the banks, they passed settlements where the people greeted them with wild yelling, hand clapping, feet stomping, bodies swaying, eyes rolling, and drums beating. Marlow admitted an inner response to this passionate uproar, but he was too busy keeping his "tinpot" steamer afloat to go ashore for a "howl and a dance."

Fifty miles below Kurtz' station, they came upon an abandoned hut where a supply of fresh firewood was stacked. Here, Marlow found a book. It had no cover, but to Marlow it seemed the only real object he had found on the trip. The delays were many, but the manager displayed "a beautiful resignation."

A mile and a half below the Inner Station, an attack took place and the steamer was showered with arrows. A spear thrown through the pilothouse window fatally wounded the black helmsman. In great fright, the manager ordered Marlow to turn back, but before Marlow could comply with the order, the Inner Station came in sight.

A curiously dressed Russian welcomed them. He proved to be

Kurtz' disciple and devotee. He told Marlow that Kurtz was very ill but still alive. The manager and his pilgrims went up to the house to bring Kurtz to the steamer. Marlow talked to the Russian and learned that Kurtz ordered the attack on the steamer. Kurtz had been without trade goods for many months, yet he had collected ivory at gunpoint until he had a huge supply. He had become a god among the natives. They worshipped him, and he participated in their horrible, secret rites. He had even tried to shoot the Russian, who had nursed him through two nearly fatal illnesses.

The men brought Kurtz down to the steamer on an improvised stretcher. He was scarcely more than a cadaver, yet his voice was strong. The shore was filled with natives who did not want their "deity" to leave. Among them was a magnificent black woman – "savage and superb."

That night, Kurtz escaped and crawled back toward a savage devil ceremony in the jungle. Marlow went after him and brought him back, but not before he had glimpsed the vile and "inconceivable" degradation of the man's soul.

Kurtz entrusted Marlow with a packet of private papers. A few days later, Kurtz died with a final cry, "The horror! The horror!" The next day, the pilgrims buried him in a muddy hole.

Afterward, Marlow became sick and was shipped back to Europe. There, three persons called on him, inquiring about Kurtz' papers. One was a company officer, another was a musician who claimed to be Kurtz' cousin, and a third was a journalist. Marlow told them that Kurtz' papers were of no value and that he was saving them for Kurtz' "Intended."

Later, at her door, Marlow was almost overcome with a vision of the dying Kurtz, his mouth open voraciously as though to devour the whole world. The awful cry, "The horror! The horror!" rang all around him. Marlow entered and met the girl – beautiful, pale, and robed in black. She was filled with terrible and deep agony over her loss. Her words revealed that she held Kurtz to be the most noble of men – honest, lovable, faithful, and true.

For a long time, Marlow answered her evasively. At last, though, he said that he had heard Kurtz' last words. She demanded to know them, and Marlow lied to the girl. He assured her that her name was the last word on Kurtz' lips. The girl's loud cry of exultation, of "inconceivable triumph and of unspeakable pain," and her subsequent weeping showed Marlow that healing tears had come at last. By his lie, Marlow freed the girl from her agony, and she could now make a healthy recovery. As Marlow left the house, he half-expected the heavens to fall in retribution for his lie – but nothing happened.

The listeners on the deck of the *Nellie* respond rather insensitively to Marlow's story. The narration of the novel returns to the unnamed narrator, who describes Marlow as sitting "apart, indistinct, and silent, in the pose of a meditating Buddha." The book ends, as it began, with an allusion to the Thames – "the tranquil waterway leading to the uttermost ends of the earth flowed sombre under an overcast sky – seemed to lead into the heart of an immense darkness."

INTRODUCTION TO THE NOVEL

The novel has a "framed" narrative structure, meaning that one "I" opens the story and sets the stage for the second "I," who narrates the tale. The first "I" speaks in first-person objective; the second "I" (Conrad-Marlow) speaks in first-person subjective.

The story comes out of its frame and returns to the *Nellie*'s deck several times. Conrad's object in providing these "returns" is to show Marlow's audience and its lack of perception. Each return entails a change of viewpoint.

As in *Lord Jim* and other of Conrad's early works, Conrad puts two or more characters' conversations into a single paragraph. Modern writers usually separate each person's speech into separate paragraphs. Many paragraphs of Conrad's are much too long. Conrad uses more punctuation than writers would use today, especially exclamation points, dashes, and dots. Marlow's story is all in quotes necessitating inner quotes for all the dialogue in the story.

Although of Polish birth, Conrad learned English thoroughly. He uses a vocabulary which any modern writer might envy. He chooses strong dramatic words. His metaphors and similes conjure up startling images. His peculiar habit of pairing adjectives occurs often in *Heart of Darkness*, as it does in *Lord Jim*. Typical examples are: "exuberant and entangled," "hospitable and festive," "empty and desolate."

Some critics object to Conrad's use of so many words which attempt to say what cannot be put into words, such as impenetrable, incredible, inextricable, inscrutable, incomprehensible, unfathomable, and most frequent of all, inconceivable. These critics feel that Conrad obscures his story with these words.

Conrad's work, however, charms his readers with its oblique approach. Examples in *Heart of Darkness* are numerous. One excellent example is the roundabout method he uses to show that the manager's excuses for neglecting Kurtz are phony. Kurtz is able to negotiate three hundred miles of the upper Congo in a dugout canoe with native rowers. His half-caste clerk is able to bring a fleet of ivory-laden canoes down the remaining seven hundred miles to the Central Station. The manager could have sent up a fleet of dugouts had he truly wished to relieve Kurtz.

Another example of the oblique approach is Conrad's having Marlow repeatedly use a single gesture: Marlow "turns away." Thus, Conrad emphasizes one of his main themes: *man's inhumanity to man is his greatest sin.* Note that in every instance where Marlow *turns away,* he is witness to senseless cruelty. Conrad uses this oblique approach to show, through the attitude of Marlow's four listeners, another of his themes: *materialistic minds cannot grasp, or be interested in, adventures of the spirit.*

SUMMARIES AND COMMENTARIES

SECTION 1

Summary

The *Nellie,* a two-masted sailboat, swings at anchor in the Thames River outside London, waiting for the turn of the tide. Five Englishmen lounge on her deck: the owner of the boat, a lawyer, an accountant, Marlow, and the narrator (the first "I" of this framed narrative). The accountant brings out his dominoes, but the men do not play. Instead, they contemplate the mighty river at sunset, staring into the gauzy, radiant lights of London reflected on the river's rippling surface.

The narrator of this novel tells us that Marlow is the only one present who still "follows the sea"; Marlow is a "wanderer," and he sits cross-legged, Buddha-like, leaning against the mizzenmast (the shorter mast). Suddenly, as the rest of the men are delighting in the brilliantly reflected lights of civilized London, Marlow blurts out, "And this also has been one of the dark places of the earth." No one says anything. Marlow continues, speaking very slowly about the civilized Romans who came to conquer the wild, untamed British Isles years ago. He pictures their hardships – the cold, fog, tempests, disease, death, and their encounters with the savage natives – all of which must have been the Roman soldiers' lot as they felt the immense, dark abomination of Celtic England closing in around them.

The "fascination of abomination" obsesses Marlow; he imagines a conquering Roman's "longing to escape, his powerless disgust, his surrender and hate." Marlow says that conquerors need only brute force, a quality which is nothing to brag about because one's strength is but an accident growing out of another's weakness. Marlow denounces colonization as "robbery with violence, aggravated murder on a great scale, and men going at it blind – as is very proper for those who tackle a darkness." He sees the conquest of the earth as taking from those who "have a different complexion or slightly flatter noses." Colonization, Marlow says, can be defended only if it is carried out with a "devotion to efficiency"; that is, in order to civilize the world – not to exploit it.

Silence ensues. The men on the *Nellie*'s deck continue to gaze out at the multi-colored, flaming lights of the river traffic. They wait patiently; they can do little else until the tide turns. After a long silence, Marlow begins speaking again. He reminds his companions that once he turned freshwater sailor, and the narrator remarks that the group on the *Nellie*'s deck know that before the ebb tide begins, they are fated to listen to yet another of Marlow's "inconclusive experiences."

Marlow begins his story by jumping forward in time, describing how he ascended to the upper reaches of the river one day and met "the poor chap." He describes his experience as somber, pitiful, and not extraordinary – yet "it seemed somehow to throw a kind of light."

He begins the chronological sequence of his story, but first he tells the men that maps have always fascinated him – especially the blank spots on maps, the places that have not yet been explored. The "biggest, the most blank" space has always appealed to him. Today, however, one particular blank space is no longer blank; it is known as Africa, a place associated with darkness. Today, we also know that a great river flows through that once-blank area; this giant river, the Congo, lies like "an immense snake uncoiled, with its head in the sea, its body at rest curving afar over a vast country, and its tail lost in the depths of the land." Years ago, the snake charmed Marlow as it might charm "a silly little bird."

At the time of his story, Marlow says, he had just returned from a six-year "dose" of the Far East and, after a period of rest, he began to hunt for a new ship to sign on with. None of the ship companies wanted him, so he decided to apply to a company developing trade in the vast, dark land of Africa. He exploited his aunt's enthusiastic interest in adventure and finagled himself an appointment as the skipper of a river steamboat owned by an ivory company.

Marlow relates how the company had just received word that one of their river captains had been killed in a scuffle with the natives. He says that months later he attempted to collect the mortal remains of Fresleven, his predecessor, and found them undisturbed where the man fell, with long grass growing up through the skeleton. In addition, Marlow found the native village deserted and learned that a quarrel over two black hens ended the river captain's life. Then Marlow returns to the chronology of his story.

He quickly readied himself, and within forty-eight hours after receiving a reply from his new employers, he crossed the Channel and presented himself. Two women in the company's outer office immediately caught his attention. One was fat, the other one was thin. Both were knitting "feverishly" with skeins of black wool. On one of the office walls, a map pictured the world in rainbow colors. The yellow patch at "dead center" was Marlow's destination. The large, coiling river, the Congo, was there, fascinating and deadly.

Ushered into the manager's office, Marlow got an impression of pale plumpness behind a massive desk and was reminded of the millions of francs that this man controlled. In a few moments he had signed his contract and concluded his business. He passed through the outer office, where the two women still knitted their black wool. He felt uneasy. The white-haired secretary seemed to pity him openly, and the knitting women looked at him in a strange way.

A young compassionate clerk led Marlow out, and since it was too early to see the doctor for a medical examination, the two sat down for a drink. The young man spoke so glowingly of the company's prospects in Africa that Marlow expressed surprise that the young man himself had not gone to the outpost. The youth replied, "I am not such a fool as I look." Later, the doctor astonished Marlow by a similar comment. Measuring Marlow's head, he asked, "Ever any madness in your family?" He advised Marlow to "avoid irritation" in Africa; a calm spirit, he said, was the most vital requirement for survival in the tropics.

After a dutiful and grateful farewell to his generous aunt, Marlow was ready to leave. For a brief moment, he had a feeling of panic. Clearly, his aunt had recommended him, Charlie Marlow, as a kind of "emissary of light" who would travel from this "sepulchral city" (Brussels) to the dark continent (Africa), bringing the light and goodness of civilization. Marlow feared, however, that he was "about to set off for the center of the earth."

He left on a French steamer which traveled slowly and stopped at every French port to unload soldiers and custom house officers. Inactivity, isolation, and the monotony of the coastline all combined to depress Marlow. He felt himself held "within the toil of a mournful and senseless delusion." Occasionally Marlow heard the surf, and the sound gave him pleasure "like the speech of a brother." Sometimes black men put out from the shore in dugouts; they comforted Marlow because he saw them as natural and true "as the surf along their coast."

One day, the steamer came upon a French man-of-war ship shelling the jungle coastline. Marlow's steamer delivered mail to the man-of-war, and it was learned that the sailors aboard her were dying at the rate of three a day. The steamer sailed on, but it never stopped long enough for Marlow to get any definite impression of the African country. Wonder grew in him. He began to regard this voyage as a "pilgrimage amongst hints for nightmares."

In thirty days, the ship reached the mouth of the big river, the Congo, and because Marlow's work would be farther upstream, he took passage on a small seagoing steamer commanded by a Swedish captain who befriended Marlow and confided to him his low opinion of the colonizing agencies in the region. He said that he took a fellow Swede up the river not long ago, and the fellow hanged himself. When Marlow asked why, the captain answered evasively, "The sun too much for him, or the country perhaps."

When Marlow reached the Outer Station, the captain tied up at a jetty below a rocky hill crowned with the buildings of the ivory company—three barrack-like structures. Marlow's introduction to Africa and the ivory enterprise began here.

He started to walk up the slope toward the company buildings and discovered a boiler "wallowing in the grass," as well as a small railway truck on its back, its wheels in the air. Rusted, broken machinery and quantities of loose rails cluttered the area.

At his left was a grove of trees where dark shapes stirred feebly. Then his attention was captured by what seemed a senseless, explosive detonation and, simultaneously, an emaciated, ragged six-man chain gang clanked past, driven by an arrogant guard. Marlow was shocked by the hideous sight; he hesitated, turned his back until the chain gang was out of sight, and then he walked toward the grove.

Avoiding a vast and seemingly useless hole, Marlow almost fell into a ravine where defunct, corroded machinery and a quantity of broken drain pipes had been discarded. Then he reached the grove of trees and found himself within the "gloomy circle of some inferno." Starving, wasted human forms—black shadows of disease—crowded the grassy earth. They were scattered in every pose of "contorted collapse," resembling a picture of "a massacre or a pestilence." He noted one animated skeleton in particular—a boy who had tied a string of white cotton around his black neck. Marlow offered the boy a biscuit from the ship, and the boy accepted it, but did not taste it.

Horror-struck, Marlow made for the station at the top of the hill, and there he met a white man so elegantly dressed that he seemed almost to be a supernatural vision of white, shiny cleanliness. This "hairdresser's dummy," holding a green-lined parasol in a big white hand, was the chief accountant, the man who kept books for the ivory operation, and his office was as neat as his person. In contrast, everything else about this station was in a chaotic muddle.

Marlow was obliged to spend ten days, an eternity, at the Outer Station, and the wretched conditions outside compelled him to spend a great deal of his time inside the pale, flabby dignitary's office. Big flies continually buzzed through the air; Marlow says that they didn't sting—they "stabbed." One day, a deathly sick agent was brought in from another outpost and lay in the accountant's office. Another day, a caravan arrived, and the ensuing noise provoked the accountant into revealing his loathing for the black natives: "One comes to hate these savages—hate them to the death."

The next day, Marlow set out from the Outer Station on a two-hundred-mile inland trip to the Central Station, accompanied by sixty native carriers, each one with a sixty-pound load. A white trader also went along, a fat and sickly individual who constantly fainted in the hot sun and had to be carried.

Marlow's party met a white man who professed to be in charge of road maintenance, but Marlow saw no evidence of a road or road repair. He did find, however, a few miles farther down the trail, the body of a middle-aged black man with a bullet hole in his forehead.

After fifteen days on the difficult trek, Marlow hobbled into the Central Station. One look at the place revealed that it was as chaotic as the Outer Station, and Marlow learned immediately that the steamboat that he was supposed to command was wrecked and at the bottom of the river. Thunderstruck, he inquired, "Why? how? why?" One of the agents, a black moustached man, assured him that everything was all right. "The manager himself" had been there . . . "everyone behaved splendidly." Even now, the manager was waiting to see him.

Marlow stops his narration and says that at the time he did not realize the "real significance of the wreck," but now he understands a great deal more. At that time, however, there was little else to do except fish up his steamer from the river bottom and repair her. The job would take months.

Marlow's first interview with the manager of the Central Station proved unusual. The man knew that Marlow had walked twenty miles since dawn, but he did not ask him to sit down. The manager was a commonplace but inscrutable man with cold blue eyes and a glance that fell "as trenchant and heavy as an axe." He inspired only uneasiness. He had no learning or intelligence, and he had held his position for nine years for one reason only: his excellent health.

The manager began to speak, nervously saying that Marlow was a long time coming. Two days earlier, he had wanted to wait for Marlow, but could wait no longer; he had to set out for the Inner Station because Mr. Kurtz, the manager of the Inner Station upriver was gravely ill. Unfortunately, the skipper of Marlow's steamboat was inexperienced and tore the bottom out of Marlow's ship. Marlow said that he had already heard about Mr. Kurtz; he heard about him on the coast.

"Ah! so they talk of him down there," the manager said tensely, assuring Marlow that Kurtz was the best agent, "an exceptional man of the greatest importance to the company." The manager, still restless and apprehensive, fidgeted in his chair, exclaiming, "Ah, Mr. Kurtz!" Then he estimated that it would take three months before they could make a start to raise and repair the sunken steamboat. Marlow stormed out of the manager's hut muttering that the manager was a "chattering idiot." Outside, the "silent wilderness" struck Marlow as something "great and invincible, like evil or truth."

One evening, not long afterward, a shed full of trade goods — calico, cotton prints, beads, and such — caught fire. Marlow went to investigate and overheard two men talking. One of the men mentioned Kurtz and said something about taking advantage of "this unfortunate incident." Discovering that one of the men was the manager, Marlow sensed that an air of sinister secrecy, a breath of putrid plotting hung over everything at the Central Station.

A young agent — a brickmaker who as yet had made no bricks — invited Marlow to his room, where he tried to pump Marlow about his influential friends and supporters in Europe (by "Europe," he meant Belgium; remember that at the time of the story, this area of Africa was known as the Belgian Congo). Marlow was amazed and disgusted. He rose to leave, but noticed a small sketch done in oils on a panel. The painting was of a blindfolded woman carrying a lighted torch. The background was dark, and the effect of the torchlight on her face was sinister.

The agent held up a candle so Marlow could see the painting better. He explained that Mr. Kurtz painted the picture more than a year ago, when he was here at the Central Station. Marlow asked with genuine interest, "Who is this Mr. Kurtz?" The agent said that Marlow and Kurtz were alike, that both of them were men who belonged to a "new gang of virtue," men who hoped to bring "pity and science and progress" (metaphorically, light) to darkest Africa. The agent was sure that Marlow must know of the company's plans for Kurtz. Marlow laughed and asked if the agent read the company's private correspondence. The man did not answer. "When Mr. Kurtz is general manager," Marlow said in a severe voice, "you won't have the opportunity."

The agent then snuffed out the candle, and the two men went out into the night, where they met the man with the black moustache. He commended whoever was beating the black native who was blamed for the fire; in the darkness, a voice groaned. The moustached man growled, "Transgression — punishment — bang! Pitiless, pitiless. That's the only way."

Marlow observed the forest standing like a specter in the moonlight. Its mystery, its immense, profound greatness, and the amazing reality of its concealed life took ever-deeper roots in Marlow's heart.

The agent followed Marlow and persisted in trying to explain his own attitude toward Mr. Kurtz. He didn't want Marlow to take a bad report to Kurtz; he insisted that Marlow was in the same class as Kurtz, and that *he,* as a brickmaker, could be helpful to both Kurtz and Marlow. Marlow finally allowed him to believe what he pleased about him and Kurtz.

At this point, the story returns to the deck of the *Nellie.* Marlow's sudden silence seems difficult to explain. The narrator thinks perhaps that the other men who have been listening are now asleep. He, however, is not; he is wide awake and listening for some clue that will reveal why Marlow's tale makes him uneasy. Night has fallen, and Marlow's narration is now only a disembodied voice in the darkness.

Marlow continues his story of the "papier mâché Mephistopheles" who followed him to the river bank and insisted on talking. He let the brickmaker prattle on about Kurtz for awhile, and then he turned sharply and demanded rivets so that he could repair the steamboat. By sheer coincidence, the agent said, Kurtz wanted rivets too. Marlow said that because the agent did secretarial duty for the manager, he could certainly include rivets in his regular weekly order. The agent said, however, that as a secretary, he ordered *only what he was dictated to order.* Marlow suggested that a smart fellow would find a way. The agent changed the subject and soon left.

Without rivets, Marlow could not repair the steamer, and, at present, his only interest was the steamer. Marlow comments that he doesn't like work any better than other men, but that he likes what is *in* work – "the chance to find oneself . . . your own reality."

Marlow returned to his steamboat that had been raised by now (his "battered, twisted, ruined, tinpot steamboat") and talked to the foreman, a friend of Marlow's, but a man despised by the "pilgrims" (the several agents who wandered around doing little, but always carrying long staffs). Marlow liked the foreman (a boilermaker by trade) because the man worked – and work is a prime virtue in Marlow's code of values. Marlow told him that they might get rivets, perhaps in three weeks, and the boilermaker was ecstatic. "Like lunatics," the two men performed an impromptu, clattering dance on the steamer's deck.

But the rivets did not arrive. Instead, during the next three weeks, an exploring party, the Eldorado Exploring Expedition arrived, riding on donkeys with a mass of provisions borne on the backs of footsore, sulky blacks. So disorganized was the band that it seemed to be a "mess of things . . . like the spoils of thieving." The leader of this band was the manager's uncle, a pot-bellied fellow who resembled "a butcher in a poor neighborhood." He spoke to no one but his nephew.

Commentary

The first paragraphs of this section frame what is traditionally referred to as a "framed" or "framework" story. Such a story always opens with a narrator who speaks in first person. This first "I" lays a suitable foundation for another "I" (Marlow here) who will take up the story.

Note how the author sets the mood of the story with such words as "red," "dark," "mournful," "brooding," "sombre," "hate," "murder," and many others. Everything about the opening is significant – the time: night; the lights: "A great stir of them"; Marlow's pose: Buddha-like (in meditation); flood tide: an opportune time; profession of listeners: materialistic; and the location: a ship's deck.

The reference to Roman colonization also sets the pattern for the course of Marlow's story. The tragedy of the early Roman settlers in England will be given a modern setting in Marlow's revelation. The philosophy of conquest "by right of might" is strikingly modern. "The fascination of abomination" will continue until the story's end.

Marlow's statement that his somber and pitiful contact with Kurtz "throws a kind of light" is important. The symbolism of *light* appears often in *Heart of Darkness.* One of Conrad's themes is illustrated in Kurtz' painting – that is: blindfolded lightbearers destroy what they profess to enlighten. The frequent references to "fierce sunlight" throughout the novel develop this theme.

Several other symbols mentioned in this section include the yellow patch on the map; yellow probably denotes ivory, also corruption. The comparison of the Congo to a snake foreshadows the deadly dangers which Marlow will encounter in Africa. The knitters of black wool refer to the mythological Fates weaving their black pall.

Note, too, the pitying attitude of the secretary in Brussels; it suggests her feeling that the man before her (Marlow) is doomed. Marlow's own apprehensions are also suggestive. Note his reference to Brussels, the "white sepulchral city," and his statements, "a queer feeling came to me that I was an imposter" and "an eerie feeling came over me." Note also his remark that he felt as though he were about to undertake a journey to "the center of the earth." For years, the center of the earth has been identified with hell.

In all his works, Conrad makes frequent references to the Scriptures. He draws many figures of speech and some of his most important themes from the Bible. The term "white sepulchral" is such a reference. The remainder of this text says, "full of dead men's bones." The implication is that the flourishing ivory trade, "the biggest thing" in the city, is a death-dealing operation full of dead men's skeletons.

Throughout the novel, you should be aware that Conrad is building a mood of unhealthy darkness, hopeless stupidity, senseless cruelty, avid greed, and unholy ambition. He never allows the reader to forget the direction and focus of the story. At every turn, he sees some evidence of a monstrous evil at work in the land.

Life in the Congo is difficult and dangerous – even for the exploiters themselves. Conrad continually emphasizes the heavy price which the land demands because of the invasion of its secrets and the looting of its treasures. The Swede's unaccountable suicide underlines these dangers. The dying seamen onboard the French man-of-war suggest that France shares the booty, as well as the punishment for the rape of the African continent.

Conrad uses his graphic portrayal of waste in order to show the stupid folly that controls the ivory company's operations. He gives the reader a glimpse into the "grove of death" in order to show the cruelty practiced on the black workers because of the white man's mad and greedy rush for ivory.

Contrasted with the black horror of the dying natives is the fancy whiteness of the accountant's immaculate collars and cuffs. The color symbolism here, black and white, is interesting and unusual. Both black and white denote death. Black symbolizes physical death from starvation and cruelty; white indicates spiritual and moral death through selfishness. The white string around the starving black boy's neck has an opposite meaning and symbolizes innocence. Who is to blame for the conditions at this Outer Station? The greedy white traders.

Every person whom Marlow meets in his African venture contributes something to the plot, as well as to the overall symbolism of the story. A strong emphasis on villainy is prominent throughout this tale, but approached in Conrad's oblique manner, the full impact does not strike the casual reader because in most novels, we expect a single villain; here, Conrad is not that simple.

Marlow hears Kurtz' name for the first time from the accountant, who commends Kurtz and triggers Marlow's interest in him. Then, throughout the remainder of the novel, Marlow's desire to see and talk with Kurtz grows. Perhaps Marlow senses a unity of ideal and purpose between himself and Kurtz. His identification with Kurtz progresses from his first knowledge to his final disillusionment.

Many people have been puzzled initially about the manager's discourtesy to Marlow. It stems from his fear that Marlow, like Kurtz, poses a threat to his own position. He hates Kurtz, and thus he hates Marlow, and Marlow soon realizes that the manager is intentionally delaying the shipment of any kind of help or supplies to Kurtz, who desperately needs them. The shed of trade goods probably contains supplies which should have gone to Kurtz months ago, but they burn up. Marlow correctly suspects that the manager deliberately wrecked the steamboat in order to delay Marlow from taking supplies and medicine to Kurtz.

As noted earlier, Kurtz' oil painting symbolizes the blind and stupid ivory company, personified by the manager of the Central Station, fraudulently letting people believe that besides the ivory he is taking out of the jungle, he is, at the same time, bringing light and progress to the jungle. The painting is significant for another reason, too. Its existence proves that Kurtz knows and understands clearly the nature of the company, as well as his own relation to it. He understands his own inability to carry out his fine ideals. He knows what he is doing when he plunges into the darkness of pagan rituals and allows himself to be worshipped as a god.

The agent's talk with Marlow reveals his own ambition to become assistant manager at the Central Station, and Marlow's severe pronouncement that the agent will not be allowed to snoop into company correspondence when Kurtz gets to be manager almost certainly proves to the "papier mâché Mephistopheles," as Marlow calls him, that Marlow knows Kurtz' plans and those which the company has for him. He will certainly relay this information.

The attitudes of Marlow's listeners on the sailboat suggest that they are probably bored by the long story. Only the narrator is awake most of the time. Tales of spiritual adventure find slight acceptance in the ears of men who are habitually absorbed with physical adventure and material gain.

The Eldorado Exploring Expedition is based on an actual expedition – the Katanga Expedition (1890–92). Conrad weaves it into his story where it can serve the double purpose of providing yet another example of stupid, materialistic folly and, at the same time, communicating his opinion of the Katanga Expedition and showing us a typical band of reckless, disordered buccaneers, "greedy without audacity, and cruel without courage."

SECTION 2

Summary

One evening, Marlow was lying flat on his "tinpot" steamer's deck when he overheard the manager and his uncle talking as they strolled along the creek bank. They discussed Kurtz in an unfriendly way. The manager resented Kurtz, feared his influence with the company back in Europe, and he feared that Kurtz was about to be promoted to his own position of general manager. The uncle hoped that the climate – and the profound dark heart of the jungle – would take care of Kurtz.

From the snatches of conversation, Marlow gathered that Kurtz left the Inner Station and came downriver with a shipment of ivory some nine months ago. But after traveling three hundred miles, he turned around and went back upriver in a dugout canoe with four native paddlers, leaving his half-caste clerk to convey the ivory to its destination. Clearly, the two men resented Kurtz bitterly and regarded his popularity as "frightful." The half-caste clerk who brought the ivory was referred to as "the scoundrel"; it was he who reported that Kurtz was a very sick man. In addition, Kurtz' Inner Station was without medicine, supplies, trade goods, or anything else – and had been without those necessities for over nine months already.

Marlow concluded that the manager's chief grudge against Kurtz was due to Kurtz' high ideals. He even quoted Kurtz' words: "Each station should be like a beacon on the road toward better things, a center for trade, of course, but also for humanizing, improving, instructing."

The two men then discussed some person unknown to Marlow.

This stranger seemed to have unexpectedly appeared in Kurtz' territory. The manager and his uncle agreed that the fellow should be hanged; he was obviously a free-lance ivory trader and unfair competition. "Anything can be done in this country," the uncle assured his nephew, "Trust to this—I say, trust to this." The uncle then gestured toward the forest, the creek, the mud, and the river as though invoking them all in a relentless persecution of Kurtz.

Startled, Marlow leapt up. The two men knew that they had been overheard, and they vanished up the hill.

One day, the chaotically organized Eldorado Expedition headed into the wilderness, and long afterward, word came back that all the donkeys were dead. Marlow says that he never did learn the fate of "the less valuable animals"—meaning, of course, the black men on the expedition.

Marlow then jumps ahead in his story to tell us that two months elapsed from the time the repaired steamer left the Central Station until it reached Kurtz' station, the Inner Station. After this brief look ahead in his story, Marlow returns to pick up the details about his voyage up the river toward Kurtz' station.

The river seemed like a journey back into prehistoric time, "when vegetation rioted on the earth and the big trees were kings." Hippos and alligators sunned themselves on sandbanks, and myriads of islands clogged the streams and made navigation difficult. Marlow had to guess the proper channel in the river in order to avoid hidden rocks that might suddenly rip the bottom out of his tinpot steamboat. He also had to watch for suitable firewood which could be cut and kept onboard to keep the boiler going. Continually during that trip, he was busy caring for his rickety boat, yet he felt that Truth—in all that mysterious stillness—was watching him, observing his silly and often futile "monkey tricks" as he tried his best to be wise and prudent as he battled the dark Unknown.

The action then returns to the deck of the *Nellie*, and a man rebukes Marlow. "Try to be civil," a voice growls. The narrator of the novel tells us that he knew now that there was one other listener awake on the *Nellie*'s deck, listening to Marlow's strangely hypnotic tale.

Marlow then goes on with his story; he says that they were not doing too badly getting the old steamer upriver. He likens what he was doing to a blind man's driving a van over bad roads. He says that he was always aware that at any moment he might scrape the bottom of his boat—an unpardonable sin for a skipper.

At one point during the journey, twenty cannibals were enlisted to help push the steamer off sandbars and supply wood to fire the boiler. In general, Marlow has a good opinion of the cannibals, but one should listen carefully to his assessment of them. He says that they were "fine fellows in their place." Obviously, he's not too comfortable with the knowledge that they are cannibals. He says that the cannibals brought hippo meat aboard to feed themselves during the voyage, but that it soon rotted in the fierce tropical heat, and the stench was unbearable.

The manager of the Central Station was onboard the steamer, as well as three or four of the pilgrims with their ever-present long staves. As they made their way up the river, they came upon little stations where white men rushed out to welcome them with joyous shouts about ivory. Then the steamer would move on again, "like a sluggish beetle crawling on the floor of a lofty portico." For Marlow, the steamer crawled toward only one goal—Kurtz. His interest in the feared, but clearly resourceful trader had grown until he could hardly wait to see Kurtz and talk with him.

Often at night, the passengers aboard the little steamer heard the roll of drums behind the curtain of trees. Whether or not the drums meant hostility or friendship, no one knew. Threading his way through the "heart of darkness," Marlow felt that the steamer was taking them back in time for a view of prehistory. As the little vessel would round a bend, grass huts would come into view, and naked savages would tumble out of them, yelling and gyrating wildly. What Marlow saw was "black and incomprehensible frenzy."

As the natives howled, leapt in the air, and spun around, making hideous faces, Marlow realized his genetic kinship with these seemingly inhuman, uncivilized beings; he knew that if he were man enough, he had to admit that there was within him a response to the "terrible frankness of that noise." Truth was present before Marlow — Truth stripped of its cloak of time. A real man had to admit that *human* blood roared through the bodies of the frightening black men on shore.

Once more, a voice aboard the *Nellie's* deck grunts something, and Marlow answers that No, he didn't go ashore for a "howl and a dance." Marlow explains that he was too busy to do anything other than keep the makeshift steamer afloat. He had to wrap the pipes with strips of wool blankets, watch the steering and try his best to circumvent snags, as well as watch the "black savage" who served as fireman of the steamer: "To look at him was as edifying as seeing a dog in a parody of breeches and a feather hat, walking on hind legs." The black man had filed teeth and three ornamental scars on each cheek, and he believed that a terrible devil lived in the boiler and that he had to work frantically to keep the devil under control.

Some fifty miles below Kurtz' station, the steamer came upon a ruined reed hut, a flagpole, a neatly stacked woodpile, and a message penciled on a flat board. "Wood for you. Hurry up. Approach cautiously." Instinctively, Marlow knew that something was wrong up ahead.

Looking in the dismantled hut, Marlow saw that a white man had lived there not long ago. He discovered a book, *An Inquiry into Some Points on Seamanship,* and handled the volume with extreme tenderness; he enjoyed the sensation of having come upon something unmistakably real. He observed notes written in the margin – in cipher, he thought. (Later, the "cipher" turns out to be Russian.) So absorbed was Marlow that before he knew what had happened, the wood was loaded. He slipped the book into his pocket and hurried to start the steamer's engine. The manager remarked that the white man who had lived there must have been "that miserable intruder."

The steamer could scarcely make any headway against the strong, rapid currents, but the manager displayed "a beautiful resignation." In contrast, Marlow fretted and fumed and argued with himself about whether or not he would ever talk with Kurtz. In the midst of his confusion, a flash of insight came to him, and he knew that the essentials of this whole affair were "deep under the surface, beyond my reach, and beyond my power of meddling."

Two more days brought the steamer to an estimated eight miles below Kurtz' station. Marlow wanted to push on, but the manager considered navigation too dangerous: it would be advisable to wait until morning. Marlow, much irked, complied. What could another night matter after so long a time?

Sunrise revealed a thick, heavy fog all around them. At eight or nine o'clock, it lifted like a shutter, and the blazing ball of the sun could be seen. Then the shutter of fog closed down again. Marlow was already pulling in the anchor chain, but now he released it.

Before the chain stopped running, however, a loud and desolate cry arose, followed by a savage, complaining clamor as though the mist itself were screaming from all sides. The tumult culminated in an outburst of fearful shrieking which stopped short in a silence as appalling as the noise. The terrified pilgrims rushed for their guns.

The black crew, however, grinned as they hauled the anchor chain up. The headman said, "Catch 'im. Give 'im to us." He flashed his sharp teeth. "Catch 'im!" He explained that the cannibals were hungry; they wanted to eat those noisemakers.

Marlow was at first repelled, but then he realized that the cannibals were hungry—very hungry. The voyage had lasted almost two months, and he remembered that the crew had not eaten any food except the rations brought onboard, plus a quantity of hippo meat that had soon rotted and was thrown overboard. Marlow recalled that the savages occasionally gnawed on some dirty, lavender-colored lumps wrapped in leaves.

Marlow knew that each crewman's wages amounted to three nine-inch lengths of brass wire per week. The supposition was that the men would buy food at the villages they passed, but they could rarely do that because the manager did not find it convenient to stop. Yes, Marlow knew for a certainty that the crew must be starving, and he wondered why the cannibals didn't eat the five white men onboard. They certainly could have overpowered them. Marlow decided that the white men probably looked too unappetizing to tempt even a starving savage. Then the thought occured to him that perhaps he had a touch of fever, another of the "playful paw-strokes of the wilderness."

The manager spoke suddenly, saying that he would be "desolated" if anything had happened to Mr. Kurtz. Marlow was sure that the man meant what he said. He would do anything—or say anything—to preserve appearances. He even suggested that they go on at once, but both Marlow and the manager knew that any forward movement was impossible in the heavy fog. Nevertheless, the manager's suggestion sounded good. The manager authorized Marlow to take all risks of going forward—regardless of the fog. Marlow refused, however, and turned away. "Will they attack, do you think?" the manager asked. Marlow didn't think the natives would attack them. Somehow, listening to the howling tumult in the bush, he seemed to sense that the noise sounded more sorrowful than warlike.

When the fog lifted, Marlow was able to steer the steamer in close to the bank, where the water was deepest. Marlow had one of the black crew sounding (measuring) the passage with a long pole. He saw the pole showing more and more length sticking out of the water. In an instant, the man with the pole dropped flat on the steamer's deck, and Marlow saw the fireman take shelter behind the furnace and duck his head. Arrows began to fly thick and fast over the steamer, and the black helmsman steered such a crooked course that Marlow reproved him. Then the native dropped the tiller and grabbed a rifle. The next moment he fell, fatally injured by a shafted spear. The helmsman fell at Marlow's feet, and his blood filled Marlow's shoes.

Looking up from the dead helmsman, Marlow's first remark was that Kurtz must be dead. As he tugged madly to loosen his shoes, he realized that disappointment had struck him like a physical blow. Now he would never hear Kurtz. He had always thought of Kurtz as a gifted orator, and his obsession to meet the man was based on the fact that he wanted to hear Kurtz' voice. He knew that Kurtz had "collected, bartered, swindled, or stolen more ivory than all the other agents together," but this knowledge seemed beside the point. Kurtz was a gifted creature, and the sum of all his gifts was his ability to talk well.

Marlow threw his bloody shoes into the river. His wild disappointment over not being able to see or hear Kurtz had the same quality of extravagant and howling sorrow that he had heard earlier in the cries of the savages in the bush.

Marlow defends himself at this point and says that Yes, of course, he was wrong – the privilege of hearing Kurtz' voice *did* actually await him, but at that time, he didn't know it. At that time, he had heard too many voices and too many sordid, savage noises. Then he was silent for a long time.

When Marlow resumes his tale, he jumps ahead to mention a woman whom he refers to as "Kurtz' Intended" – that is, the woman who lived in Europe and hoped to marry Kurtz when he returned – rich and successful. Marlow also describes Kurtz; he says that the man was bald, that his head was like an ivory ball, as if the wilderness had "patted him on the head . . . caressed him . . . loved him, embraced him" – and he had withered. It had "sealed his soul to its own."

Kurtz had collected a great quantity of ivory, heaps of it, stacks of it. His old mud shanty was bursting with it, and when loaded onboard the steamer, the ivory filled her hold, and piles of it had to be stacked on the deck, where Kurtz gloated over it.

Marlow pauses here to philosophize about the effect of solitude and silence on a man's "untrammelled feet." With no policemen, no neighbors, no checks at all on his behavior, a man had to fall back on his own resources of strength and faithfulness. Of course, a man may be such a fool that he doesn't even know that he is being "assaulted by the powers of darkness." However, Kurtz was no fool. He knew what he was doing.

Marlow discovered that Kurtz had written a report for the Society for the Suppression of Savage Customs. The seventeen pages of eloquence and beautiful writing – magnificent, persuasive, but without any practical hints – was postscripted by an unsteady scrawl, "Exterminate all the brutes!" Kurtz eventually entrusted this document to Marlow's care.

Kurtz was not a common man, Marlow says. He had the power to charm or frighten primitive people into compliance with his slightest wish and to exalt himself to the position of a deity among them. He frightened the pilgrims, but he had one devoted friend, and he had conquered one soul that was neither primitive nor selfish. Marlow questions, though, whether Kurtz was worth the life they lost in getting to him – namely, the black helmsman.

Marlow now leaves off his "flash-forward," and he returns to describe the dead helmsman. Although the fellow had been an inefficient sailor, Marlow realized that a subtle bond of brotherhood had existed between them. He describes how he pulled the spear from the dead man's side, observed the hungry, waiting looks on the faces of the cannibal crew, and resolved that only the river fish should have a chance to feast on the corpse. He lifted the man, dragged him to the rail, and dumped him overboard.

Marlow says that the killing frightened the manager. He favored turning back downriver at once, but Marlow suddenly looked up and saw the buildings of the Inner Station come into view around the river's bend. The manager was astonished and clapped his hands in wonder. Marlow looked through his field glasses and saw a hill sprinkled sparsely with trees and topped by a long-decaying building, half-buried in tall grass. A fence had once surrounded the house, but it had now fallen into ruin and only a few stakes remained to mark its line. Each stake was ornamented with a round, curved ball, and around the cleared slope and the dilapidated house, the forest made a tight background. The river bank was clear, and a white man under a cartwheel-like hat came toward them. At the same time, Marlow saw human forms gliding through the green tangle of jungle. The manager screamed that they were being attacked, but the white man's cheerful voice shouted a welcome.

Marlow was interested in the white stranger. He looked like a harlequin. His clothes were covered with patches and bindings of every color, making him look youthful. His boyish face was fair with no features to speak of, little blue eyes, and an open countenance which changed with his moods "like sunshine and shadow on a wind-swept plain."

When the manager and the pilgrims, all "armed to the teeth," went up to Kurtz' house, the white man came onboard. From his confused rattle of talk, Marlow gathered that he was a Russian — the son of an arch-priest — who had ventured into the jungle alone with as much idea of what might happen to him as a baby. He had wandered the river for two years and was devoted to Kurtz.

The Russian declared that Kurtz had "enlarged" his mind and ex-plained that the natives were simple people who meant no harm; they didn't want Kurtz to leave. He advised Marlow to keep enough steam in his boiler so that he could blow the whistle if necessary — noise would do more good than rifles.

Marlow gave the book that he found in the deserted house to the Russian, who was ecstatic with joy. He believed that the book had been lost.

Commentary

The conversation that Marlow overhears establishes the follow-ing important points regarding Kurtz and the manager:
1. The manager fears and hates Kurtz.
2. The manager has purposely delayed and avoided sending both food and supplies to Kurtz, hoping that his illness would be-come worse and he would die.
3. The manager's defense of his neglect of Kurtz is false and in-valid. If Kurtz could manage the three hundred miles of the river alone in a dugout with four native paddlers, the manager could have sent supplies up to him by the same means at any time.
4. Even the abundant flow of previous ivory from Kurtz' Inner Station infuriates the manager. He knows that such success will endear Kurtz to the company.

5. Marlow's impulsive reaction to the revelation of the manager's inhuman treatment of Kurtz shows his horror at such conduct. Also, he knows that he is classed with Kurtz. What vicious plot will the manager concoct to get rid of him, the new steamer captain? No wonder Marlow leaps up in horror.

Throughout this novel, Marlow will mention Truth. Truth in Marlow's philosophy may be good *or* evil. Truth has two sides: the dark truth and the light truth – the black truth and the white truth. The reproving and mocking voices that interrupt Marlow are proof of how little the materialistic listeners aboard the *Nellie* comprehend Marlow's spiritual quest.

Note continually in this section how Marlow's interest in Kurtz grows. It has become an obsession. Marlow's response to the frenzied howling in the jungle reveals Marlow's own "dark truth." *He is conscious of his own wild and savage potential.*

The manager's "beautiful resignation" when the little tinpot steamer can barely make progress through the fierce rapids is an example of Conrad's understatement. Marlow knows that the manager *would* – even now – *were it possible*, prevent by some means any relief from reaching Kurtz.

In addition, the manager's innate cruelty and unspeakable inhumanity are proof of his prejudice against the black crew. He knows that they have no food, and although he provides wages of brass wire, he makes no provision for them to use it in trading.

Marlow's lengthy comments on the amazing restraint of the blacks is important. One of the questions raised in this story is: "What restraints prevent a man from yielding to his dark compulsions?" His philosophical reflections show that, in his opinion, the blacks exhibit more civilized self-control than the whites onboard.

The character of the young Russian man is an odd element in the story. Conrad seems to insert him in order to present a fool, a man too blockheaded to know when he is assaulted by the powers of darkness. His rattlebrained talk reveals how dangerous Kurtz has become, but seemingly the Russian is blindly devoted to Kurtz.

When the manager and his guard of pilgrims go up to Kurtz' house, note that they are heavily armed. They are a bunch of frightened cowards who do not care about the dying Kurtz. The ivory in his mud storehouse is their only interest. For the ivory, they will risk anything.

SECTION 3

Summary

Marlow marveled at this strange Russian whose existence was beyond reason. For months, even years, this man's life hadn't been worth a day's wage, and yet here he was—gallantly and thoughtlessly alive. The Russian urged Marlow to take Kurtz away, "Quick—quick—I tell you." Marlow contemplated the mystery of the young man because he was so utterly selfless; he wanted nothing from the wilderness but breathing space. Marlow judged that the young man's acceptance of and devotion to Kurtz were the most important—but certainly the most dangerous—things that had happened to him.

As the Russian threw up his arms in a gesture of enthusiasm for the enlightenment which Kurtz had given him, Marlow saw the headman of the black woodcutters turn heavy, glittering eyes on the fair youth, and Marlow was afraid.

Marlow soon discovered that the Russian's friendship with Kurtz had been disconnected rather than continuous. The young man had nursed Kurtz through two serious illnesses. Kurtz had wandered for long periods deep in the forest and had discovered many villages— the young man did not know in what direction. Kurtz simply went out for ivory. When Marlow reminded the young man that Kurtz had no goods to trade for ivory, the Russian said, "There's a good lot of cartridges left even yet."

In other words, Marlow said, Kurtz "raided the country" for his ivory. The young Russian agreed, but he said that the people in the villages adored Kurtz. Kurtz came to them with thunder and lightning. They had never seen anything like it. The Russian told Marlow, "You can't judge Mr. Kurtz as you would an ordinary man." All the while the Russian was talking, Marlow realized that there was a multitude of people hidden in the bush.

The young man said that Kurtz was gravely ill, and Marlow took up his field glasses and turned them on Kurtz' house. He discovered that the ornamental knobs which decorated Kurtz' fence were dried black heads. Marlow wondered about those heads; they were proof that there was something Marlow had never dreamed of beneath Kurtz' legendary "magnificent eloquence." Marlow realized that the wilderness had whispered things to Kurtz, and that the whisper had proved irresistibly fascinating. "It echoed loudly within him because he was hollow at the core."

The Russian, perturbed by Marlow's words, explained that no one dared to remove the dried black heads. They were symbols, and Mr. Kurtz' word was law. His ascendance was "extraordinary." The Russian began to tell Marlow how the native chiefs crawled in Kurtz' presence, but Marlow shut him up. This revelation struck Marlow as being even more intolerable than the sight of native heads drying on stakes under Kurtz' windows. The Russian explained that these heads belonged to "rebels," and he tried with sincere emotion to defend Kurtz. This kind of life, he said, tries a man; Kurtz had been shamefully abandoned: there hadn't been "a drop of medicine or a mouthful of invalid food" at the station for months.

Suddenly, Marlow saw a party bringing Kurtz down the slope on an improvised stretcher. They waded waist-deep in the long grass. A cry arose, piercing "the still air like a sharp arrow flying straight to the very heart of the land." Streams of people suddenly appeared. The Russian, standing at Marlow's shoulder remarked, "Now, if he does not say the right thing to them, we are all done for."

Marlow saw the men who were bearing the stretcher suddenly stop as though paralyzed, and Kurtz sat up. Marlow watched his gestures through his field glasses, but could not hear his voice. He realized that Kurtz' name meant "short" in German; he thought the name was appropriate. When Kurtz opened his mouth, it seemed as if he wanted to swallow the air, the earth, and all the people on it. Marlow heard a strong, deep voice. Then the stretcher bearers again took up their burden. The sick man lay down, and the crowd of savages vanished into the immense jungle as though it had breathed them out and breathed them in again.

The pilgrims walking behind the stretcher carried Kurtz' firearms. Kurtz was carried aboard the steamer and was laid on a couch in one of the small cabins. Kurtz looked straight into Marlow's face and said forcefully, "I am glad." These first words from Kurtz astonished Marlow; the man seemed incapable of even a whisper.

Now warriors appeared on the riverbank, and among them appeared a beautiful black woman. She came alongside the steamer, and her face had "a tragic and fierce aspect of wild sorrow." The Russian at Marlow's side growled, and the pilgrims murmured at his back. The Russian said that if the woman had tried to come aboard, he might have shot her. He said that he had risked his life for the last two weeks to keep her out of Kurtz' house. She was a mischief-maker.

Marlow heard Kurtz talking behind the curtain that served as a door to the cabin. Kurtz was saying that it was the ivory that the manager cared about – not Kurtz himself. He accused the manager of interfering with his plans and vowed that he would carry out his ideas yet – "I will return." The manager came and took Marlow aside, confiding that Kurtz was "very low." He sighed but did not show real sorrow. He tried to get Marlow to agree that they had done all they could for Kurtz, condemning Kurtz' "unsound methods"; he said that it was his duty to report these irregularities "to the proper quarter."

Marlow assured him that the brickmaker would be glad to prepare a suitable report; in his soul, Marlow was certain that he had never breathed an atmosphere so vile. He turned, mentally, to Kurtz for relief and declared aloud that Kurtz was a remarkable man. The manager dropped a "cold heavy glance" and said quietly, "He used to be." Marlow says that Kurtz was as good as buried, that even he felt buried too "in a vast grave full of unspeakable secrets . . . in the presence of victorious corruption."

The Russian then confided to Marlow that he suspected ill-will toward himself. Marlow agreed; he said that the manager thought the Russian should be hanged. The youth said that he had to get away; he couldn't do any more for Kurtz. He had friends among the savages, and there was a military station three hundred miles away. Most of all, though, he was concerned about Mr. Kurtz' reputation. Marlow assured him that Mr. Kurtz' reputation was safe. The Russian then told Marlow that Kurtz ordered the attack on the steamer because he did not want to leave his station; he thought that the attack would scare the steamer party away and convince them that he was already dead.

The Russian said that he had a canoe and three black paddlers waiting, but that he needed some cartridges. Marlow provided them, and the Russian helped himself to Marlow's tobacco and asked for shoes. Marlow gave him an old pair. Later, after midnight, Marlow woke up, sensing danger. He saw a big fire up at the corner of Kurtz' house, where an armed guard watched over the ivory. Another fire, deep within the forest, marked the spot where Kurtz' "adorers were keeping their uneasy vigil." He glanced into the room where Kurtz was. A light was burning, but Kurtz was gone. Kurtz had escaped and left the steamer.

When the full significance of this new danger came through to Marlow, he could not, at first, believe his eyes. Although one of his fellow white men slept in a deck chair not three feet away, Marlow did not awaken him. He went out alone to deal with Kurtz. He was destined, however, never to betray Kurtz, to be forever loyal to the "nightmare" of his choice.

On the bank, he picked up Kurtz' trail through the wet grass. Kurtz was crawling on all fours. Marlow was sure that he could overtake him, and soon he did. Kurtz heard him coming and rose up "like a vapor exhaled by the earth." Marlow had cut him off thirty yards from the fire. Now, he suddenly realized what would happen if Kurtz began shouting. He threatened and pleaded, but he soon realized that it would not be easy to get Kurtz back onboard the steamer. Kurtz, he realized, had "looked over the edge" and had seen the "inconceivable mystery of a soul that knew no restraint, no faith, and no fear, yet [was] struggling blindly with itself."

The next day, with Kurtz onboard, Marlow headed his steamer downriver, and again a crowd of blacks swarmed out into the open land. Among them was the magnificent black woman. To avoid trouble, Marlow pulled the cord of his whistle, and its screech scattered most of the natives. The beautiful black girl, however, did not flinch. She advanced right down to the water's edge and stretched her bare arms toward the steamer which was bearing Kurtz away. The crowd on deck – the white men onboard – got out their guns and started their "little fun," and Marlow remembers that he could see nothing but smoke.

The steamer returned down the river twice as fast as it had come up. The manager studied both Kurtz and Marlow with a satisfied glance. He was placid now. Kurtz would die, and the pilgrims didn't like Marlow. Marlow looked at Kurtz, who was unconscious, and saw him as a man sated with primitive emotions – sated with "lying fame . . . sham distinction . . . [and] all the appearances of success and power."

One day, the steamer broke down and had to tie up for repair. This delay shook Kurtz' confidence in surviving, and he gave a packet of papers and a photograph into Marlow's care. Marlow looked upon Kurtz as a man lying at the bottom of a precipice where the sun never shone, yet he had little time to give him. He had to work continually in order to keep the tinpot steamer going. In addition, Marlow himself was ill; at times, he felt that he had "the shakes too bad to stand."

One evening, coming in with a candle, Marlow found Kurtz conscious. With deep and heavy emotion, Kurtz said, "I am lying here in the dark waiting for death." Marlow saw a change come over the dying man's features—a look of pride, terror, and intense, hopeless despair. Kurtz cried out in a whisper, "The horror! The horror!"

Marlow blew out the candle and returned to his place in the mess-room, across the table from the manager. The manager lifted his head to give Marlow a questioning glance, then leaned back serenely, with a smug smile on his face. Suddenly, the manager's boy appeared at the door and announced "in a tone of scathing contempt, 'Mistah Kurtz—he dead!'"

The other white men at the table jumped up to see, but Marlow ignored both Kurtz' death and his burial, which occurred next day. The pilgrims buried him in a muddy hole by the river. Marlow was still gravely ill, and it was at this time that he went through a period of half-conscious struggling with death. He did not die, of course; instead, he found himself back in the European city where the company headquarters were located. The sight of people going about their ordinary business revolted him. His aunt tried to "nurse up" his strength, but Marlow told her that it was his imagination—not his body—that needed nursing. He could not loosen himself from Kurtz' hold. He heard that Kurtz' mother had died lately, watched over by Kurtz' faithful Intended.

In all, three people came to get the packet of papers entrusted to Marlow by Kurtz. The first was an official of the company; at first, he cajoled Marlow, then he threatened him; finally, Marlow gave him the report which Kurtz prepared for the Society for the Suppression of Savage Customs (with the final postscript torn off). The man read it and handed it back, dissatisfied. The next visitor claimed to be Kurtz' cousin. He said that Kurtz was a great musician. He too finally left after Marlow gave him a few family letters. The third inquirer was a journalist who thought that Kurtz was essentially a great politician. Marlow handed him the report, and the man said that he would publish it.

Marlow was now left alone with only the remaining papers, which he felt he had to take to Kurtz' Intended. He believed that his memory of Kurtz was no different than the memories of other men which he held in his mind, but standing before the tall door where the girl, the Intended, lived, Marlow had a distinct vision of Kurtz on the stretcher as he was brought aboard the steamer. His mouth was open in that voracious, devouring way, as though he hungered to swallow the whole world and all mankind. The vision went in the door with Marlow, accompanied by the forest gloom, and the drum beats that were the pulse of "a conquering darkness." Rushing around him, as he went into the girl's house, Marlow heard again the whispered cry, "The horror!"

In the spacious drawing room, there were three long windows, a tall marble fireplace, and a high door which opened and closed. A girl stood before him. She was all in black, her pale head floating toward him in the dusk. Marlow saw that this girl was not a plaything of time. For her, Kurtz was dying at this moment. She was suffering no ordinary grief. A conversation followed during which Marlow answered her eager questions with hesitating double-talk. Finally, he admitted that he had heard Kurtz' last words. She demanded to hear them, and Marlow lied to her. He told her that just before Kurtz died, he uttered her name.

"I knew it—I was sure!" the girl cried and then hid her face in her hands, her healing tears bursting forth. Marlow looked at her and was appalled at his lie. He half-expected the heavens to fall, but realized that the heavens did not fall for such a trifle. He says that he could not have told her the truth: "It would have been too dark—too dark altogether."

And so the tale is done. Marlow still sits apart from the men on the *Nellie's* deck, and, for a time, no one moves. Then the owner of the sailboat remarks, "We have lost the first of the ebb." The narrator of this novel then raises his head and sees a black bank of clouds; he considers the tranquil Thames River flowing gently under an overcast sky. Instinctively, he knows that even this seemingly peaceful river leads "into the heart of an immense darkness."

Commentary

Marlow's revulsion when the cannibal looks at the plump, young blue-eyed Russian stems from his knowledge of two things: (1) the headman and his fellow cannibals are starving and want to eat the youth; (2) they are hungry because of the manager's stupid cruelty.

Such inhumanity accounts for the horrors within the dark grove of death that Marlow witnessed when he first arrived.

The Russian's sketchy revelations show how terrible Kurtz, like other white men, *can* be. The drying black heads on the stakes are proof of Kurtz' dark nature – just as we have had proof of the other white men's cruelty – in particular, the black man who was beaten unmercifully for the fire when the shed of trade goods burned at the Central Station, the willful starving of the cannibal crew of the steamer, the black man on the road with a bullet hole in his forehead, the chain gang of blacks, and, as noted earlier, the "grove of death." All of these examples are part of one enormous concept of cruelty – cruelty that white men believe is largely justified because its victims are black men. It is a cruelty that resembles an octopus whose tentacles reach into every corner of the continent that is under the control of the ivory company and its general manager.

Take note of how well the manager guards the ivory. He considers Kurtz a dangerous man, but he leaves Kurtz alone and unguarded; he believes that Kurtz is dying. Kurtz is a white man, but even in the code of the white manager, he shows no compassion for Kurtz. In contrast, Marlow knows that Kurtz is a thief, a murderer, a blasphemous rogue, a shell of a man, and hollow at the core – but still Marlow turns toward him. Marlow, again and again, physically *turns away* from the manager, but he *cannot turn away* from Kurtz. The manager is truly a monster; his evil exceeds the worst that Kurtz has done. In addition, Marlow understands that much of Kurtz' behavior is related to the manager's treatment of him.

Marlow's account of his experience in discovering and pursuing Kurtz to within thirty yards of his goal is full of significant expressions, such as:

I saw the danger in its right proportions.
It was very awful.
I tried to break the spell . . .
words heard in dreams . . .
phrases spoken in nightmares . . .
But his soul was mad.
I saw the inconceivable mystery . . .

Out of this emotional puzzle, a few certainties appear. Marlow fears that Kurtz intends to shout and bring down the whole crowd of his "adorers" on the steamer's company. The conflict he has with Kurtz on the forest floor is of a spiritual nature, soul against soul. The words spoken are commonplace, but the implications are inconceivable in their intimation of secret horrors.

The black mistress of Kurtz is a symbolic figure and should be contrasted with his Intended, his white fiancée back in Brussels. Conrad suggests that the pilgrims shot the black woman, but he allows the readers to draw their own conclusions.

Eventually, one must wonder how Marlow managed to escape the Congo – especially when we know how much hatred the manager had for him. No doubt the manager could have neglected Marlow with fatal consequences, as he did Kurtz. Perhaps two such deaths, almost simultaneous, might not give the proper impression of the ivory outpost to the Brussels office. The manager would not dare take a chance and get rid of Marlow too. Thus, indirectly, Marlow may owe his life to Kurtz, who did him the favor of dying first.

The three men who visit Marlow on his return to Brussels contribute to the truth about Kurtz. Such a versatile and gifted man has more than one valid truth about him which the world of men will hold in memory.

When Marlow visits Kurtz' Intended, note how Conrad points out all the "tall" things in the girl's house – the high and ponderous outer door, the lofty drawing room, the three long windows, the tall marble fireplace, the massive grand piano, and the high inner door. These symbols all denote the height and strength of this girl's love, in contrast with the low and shallow character of Kurtz and his debased end.

Recall now the hideous sight of Kurtz with his mouth open and the sound of his final cry, which struck Marlow at the same moment that he sensed the girl's grief; this contrast is created in order to show that there are two "truths" about Kurtz – his light truth and his dark truth. One truth is what Marlow knows about Kurtz; the other truth is what the girl knows.

Marlow stands in the same relation to this white girl as the pilgrims did to the black girl in the Congo. A weapon of destruction is in Marlow's hand. The weapon is Truth. He knows the black truth about Kurtz. If he were to hurl that truth at the white girl, she would perhaps be fatally wounded. Marlow must choose. He chooses to lie. In mercy, he substitutes a healing and a comforting lie.

Marlow has discovered a depth of compassion about himself that he never knew existed – all because of the lie he chose to tell. However, the Director of Companies' inane remark about having missed the turn of the tide not only shows how insensitive he is to Marlow's tale, but it also signifies a more important truth. The Director has also missed his own "turn of the tide." Those who give themselves to materialism are always left behind on spiritual explorations.

CRITICAL ESSAYS

FACTUAL ASPECTS OF THE NOVEL

Conrad went to the Congo in 1890. He reached the Outer Station at Matadi on June 13 and returned to Europe early the following November. The experiences, recorded in *Heart of Darkness,* occurred between these dates.

The manner of his obtaining his appointment, the knitting women and other persons in the Brussels office, and the voyage out to Africa are factual. Conrad intended to stay in the Congo for three years. He discovered that only seven percent of the company's employees managed to stay that long.

Mr. Gosse, a Belgian, was the "tailor's model" accountant in charge of the Outer Station. He died six months after Conrad first saw him. The fainting fat man who impeded Conrad's trek to the Central Station had actually come out with him from Brussels. His name was Prosper Harou, a Belgian. The villain of the story, the Central Station manager, was a Belgian named Camille Delcommune. Conrad's account describes his real character.

The steamer was the *Roi Des Belges,* a fifteen-ton boat. The upriver journey began on August 3, covered one thousand miles, and consumed twenty-eight days (Marlow says it took two months). The Central Station was at Kinchassa, and the Inner Station, under Kurtz' administration, was at Stanley Falls.

Kurtz' real name was Georges-Antoine Klein. He arrived in the Congo in 1888; the company appointed him chief of the Inner Station in 1890. His character and that of Kurtz were similar.

Conrad reveals his bitter disappointment over Congo affairs in letters to his aunt, Madame Marguerite Poradowska. He suffered four attacks of fever in two months as well as severe bouts with dysentery. Even the minor incidents in *Heart of Darkness* are mostly factual.

Conrad kept a diary of his Congo adventure – the only diary he ever kept.

PAIRING

Conrad uses this device in many of his works to bring out fine points of comparison and contrast, and thus he enriches his stories. People, objects, and actions are often paired. This book furnishes examples of all three.

Kurtz' *black mistress* and his *Intended* are paired for contrast as well as for comparison. The black girl wears gorgeous colors and fabulous jewelry. The white girl is draped in black. The black girl exhibits a wild and tempestuous temperament. The white girl is calm, patient, and self-possessed. Yet they both love Kurtz with a faithful-unto-death devotion.

Examples of paired objects: the small, mismatched *windows* in Kurtz' house are paired with the floor-to-ceiling *windows* in his Intended's house. The huge, stabbing *flies* that buzz over the dying agent in the accountant's office are paired with the shower of small *flies* in the messroom of the steamer at the hour when Kurtz dies. The *funeral* of the black helmsman pairs with Kurtz' *funeral*.

Examples of paired actions: the pilgrims' *shooting* of the black girl is paired with Marlow's deliberate *lie* which saves the white girl. The black girl *reaches her brown arms* after the retreating steamer. The white girl *puts out her black-draped arms* as after a retreating figure. The French man-of-war *firing* toward the coast of Africa pairs with the pilgrims *shooting* at the hippo. Both targets continue as though nothing had disturbed them.

THEMES AND PLOT

Critics have discovered many themes in *Heart of Darkness*. Some think that Conrad is talking about a man's search for self-knowledge. Certainly Marlow had no such *conscious* goal. Others see a mystical revelation of man's dark self. Still others emphasize Marlow's philosophy that work, faith, and responsibility tend to hold a man in line with civilized standards. All these meanings and many others may rightfully be accepted as threads in the texture of Conrad's most subtle work.

Study of the plot exposes only two lines of aggressive purpose.

Marlow develops such a strong purpose to see and talk with Kurtz that it becomes a life-and-death matter to him. The general manager nurses a purpose of destruction against Kurtz which is as murderous as that of the most immoral villain in any plot. Conrad is too skilled a craftsman to have failed in the most vital part of his plot structure. People would not enjoy this book if it had been written around a weak plot. No strong plot has ever been written without powerful and aggressive purpose on the part of both hero and villain.

Since the book closes with a *lie* which is, in reality, an affirmation of the truth, perhaps Conrad's chief purpose in this story is the discovery and analysis of the double aspects of truth – black truth and white truth, which are both inherent in every human soul. An analysis of the manager's reason for destroying Kurtz shows that at every turn, he works to prevent the truth from being known. Should the company in Belgium find out the truth about Kurtz' success as an ivory procurer, or discover his multiplicity of talents, they would certainly elevate him to the position of manager at once. The manager's insidious and pretending nature opposes all truth.

On the opposite side of the struggle, Marlow seeks affirmation of truth. It is Kurtz' voice he wants to hear, Kurtz' words. His search is for the "inner truth." More and more he identifies with Kurtz, and, in the end, "it is his extremity" that Marlow goes through. Like the Captain in *The Secret Sharer* who finds his dark self in Leggatt, Marlow finds in Kurtz his own dark self. Throughout the book, the black people typify truth and reality. They have "white souls" while the rapacious whites have black souls. Compare the cannibals' restraint (though starving, they do not attack their white persecutors) with Kurtz' *lack* of restraint.

Conrad also deals in this story with the lure of the abyss – the acrophobia of the soul. The manager and his fellows leap into the abyss, Kurtz is pushed in, while Marlow is drawn to the edge, near enough to "look over," but habits of integrity, responsibility, and a settled faith pull him back. A quote from Charles Dickens, in *A Tale of Two Cities*, expresses the truth Marlow discovers:

> In seasons of pestilence some of us will have a secret attraction to the disease – a terrible passing inclination to die of it. And all of us have like wonders hidden in our breasts, only needing circumstances to evoke them.

The reason many persons never fall into depravity is, perhaps, because the evoking circumstance never arrives.

The following themes, both positive and negative, are some of those which appear in *Heart of Darkness:*

- Man's inhumanity to man is his greatest sin.
- A man's confrontation with his dark self is both dangerous and enlightening.
- Every soul has its dark truth and its light truth – in short, the potential for degradation or nobility.
- The material-minded person cannot understand or follow spiritual quests or adventures into the spirit.
- Blindfolded bearers of light destroy what they profess to enlighten.
- Removal of all restraints in solitude and silence will bring out a man's true nature.
- The strongest barrier to the abyss is a previous commitment to faith and responsibility.

COLOR SYMBOLISM

In this novel, black and white have the usual connotations of evil and good. Throughout the book the *white* souls of the black people are contrasted with the *black*-souled whites who exploit them. The *white* string of cotton around the starving *black* boy's neck in the "grove of death" sets the symbol for the story. The *white* colors and cuffs worn by the accountant are phony; the man is *black* with hatred inside.

The women in the Belgian company's office knit *black* wool, a symbol of dark fate and tragedy to follow. Marlow's predecessor dies because of a quarrel over two *black* hens. The heads on Kurtz' fence are *black*. The background of Kurtz' oil painting is *black*. The peak of Kurtz' broken roof contains a yawning *black* hole.

Yellow symbolizes cowardice and also corruption, putrification, and decay. *Yellow* marks the Congo area on the map in the Brussels office. It also symbolizes the *yellow* ivory.

The *multicolored* patches and trimmings on the Russian's harlequin clothes symbolize his changing moods and his light-hearted, foolish nature.

The *pale* look of the ivory company's manager denotes death. The Bible uses the *pale* symbol in Revelations 6:8: the "pale horse" and his rider, "Death." Note that the Intended looks *pale*; she is dying of grief until Marlow "saves" her with a lie.

OBJECTS AS SYMBOLS

The *jungle* symbolizes truth and reality. *Grass* is referred to in many places. *Grass* grows up through Fresleven's skeleton. The rusted and wasted tools and equipment at the Outer Station lie in the *grass*. Marlow's trek to the Central Station lies through burnt *grass,* past *grass* huts, and he discovers a dead native in the *grass* along the path. The shadows of the noxious general manager and his uncle trail shadows behind them that do not bend a blade of the tall *grass*. Kurtz' house is half-buried in tall *grass*. The carriers wade through waist-high *grass* to bring Kurtz' litter down to the steamer. The meaning of the *grass* symbolism is probably that of the Scripture – ". . . they are like the grass: in the morning, it flourisheth; in the evening, it is cut down and withereth." (Psalm 90). In other words, men's wickedness, as well as their goodness, is transient. Like grass it springs and fades.

Blinding sunshine referred to in many places symbolizes the pitiless persecution taking place under the guise of enlightenment. The *stick of sealing wax* which the manager breaks while he is talking about Kurtz symbolizes Kurtz, and the manager breaks it just as he longs to break Kurtz. The *rivets* which prove so hard to get symbolize all the important and practical things that are omitted from the general manager's program.

The *huge buzzing flies* stabbing the dying agent in the accountant's immaculate office symbolize, in general, the operations of the ivory company's representatives – specifically, the pilgrims. They also symbolize Marlow's reaction to Congo conditions. The *swarm of small flies* which stream upon everything in the messroom of the steamer at the time Kurtz dies should be contrasted with the big flies. One swarm comes into the story's beginning, the other at its end. Conrad never introduced such twined effects without meaning something important. Perhaps the flies symbolize the irritation Marlow feels over the annoyances he meets in the Congo. At first, they seem enormous; later, they diminish because of his growth in character.

The *pail with a hole in it* which the fat agent uses to fight the fire symbolizes the inadequacy of all the pilgrims and hangers-on at the Central Station. *Candles* symbolize light – feeble light.

The *oil painting* proves that Kurtz understands the situation at the

Central Station, that he knows how stupid and blind the company representatives are, and that he plunges into darkness and degradation with his eyes open. The painting brings out another theme: blindfolded bearers of light destroy what they profess to enlighten.

Shoes are mentioned often enough that the reader wonders what they signify. Marlow flings his bloody shoes into the river. The Russian begs Marlow for a pair of shoes. Kurtz' packet of papers is tied with a shoestring. Perhaps they symbolize protection, or guidance, or both.

SUGGESTED ESSAY TOPICS

1. Using Section 1 of the novel, draw a diagram and describe a "framed" narrative.

2. In the scene when Marlow is in the European office of the ivory company, discuss the significance and the symbolism of (1) the knitting women and their black wool; (2) the yellow patch on the map, and (3) the manager's pale plumpness.

3. Snake symbolism is used several times. Cite the instances and explain the symbolism.

4. Discuss the significance of the forest.

5. Why does the manager think that Marlow is like Kurtz?

6. Discuss Kurtz' treatment of the Russian – humane or cruel?

7. Contrast Kurtz' black mistress with his Intended.

8. Explain why Marlow lies to Kurtz' Intended.

9. Discuss Kurtz' postscript of hate on his manuscript.

10. Why does Conrad not identify either the Congo or Africa by name?

SUGGESTED ESSAY TOPICS

THE SECRET SHARER
Notes

INTRODUCTION TO THE NOVEL

Conrad suffered the loss of both parents during his childhood. Sensitive and naturally introspective, he seems never to have escaped his early sadness. Much of his writings deal with a lonely person who, for some reason, is cut off from his fellow men. The nameless Captain of *The Secret Sharer* is such a man. He feels himself a stranger among the crew of his ship. When his "other self" appears as the murderer, Leggatt, he is in a frame of mind to accept him. Later, he seems to feel that Leggatt *is* his own "dark self."

Conrad says that the incident he used for *The Secret Sharer* is true and happened on a vessel cruising in the Far East. He admits that he often saw the Captain when he was ashore in an English seaport.

Conrad wrote *The Secret Sharer* in 1909, ten years after *Heart of Darkness*. Contrast the technique used in the two stories to show how much Conrad learned in ten years from his editors and fellow writers. *Heart of Darkness* follows the old method of long sentences, overabundant punctuation, and over-written paragraphs of ponderous length. Quotes within quotes confuse the reader, and long, indefinite words mystify him.

The Secret Sharer has a modern format. The pages look inviting, and all the dialogue is set apart in separate paragraphs. The plot moves along with simple but expressive words and without excessive comments or frequent metaphors.

The many characters Conrad thought it necessary to use in *Lord Jim, Heart of Darkness,* and other of his earlier works do not clutter *The Secret Sharer*. There are two main characters, and only one is named. The psychological plot weaves itself so closely about these two that the few minor characters serve little purpose but to provide background.

The story is told from the point of view of the young, unnamed Captain of the nameless ship; the first-person subjective viewpoint allows the reader into the Captain's mind and encourages identification between protagonist and reader early in the story.

The soul-searching nature of the Captain's problem makes for frequent passages of exposition and introspection; yet the story moves along in a bright and interesting way. Even the story-within-a-story, where Leggatt relates the circumstances of his crime, does not confuse the reader nor detract from the story interest.

LIST OF CHARACTERS

Two characters carry the plot of *The Secret Sharer*, the Captain and Leggatt. Other minor characters are the *Sephora's* Skipper, the whiskery chief mate, the cocky second mate, the steward who tends the Captain's cabin, and the other crew members.

The Captain

He is a nameless Captain on a nameless ship. Conrad must have considered his story so universal that the Captain may represent every man, and the ship may symbolize the ship of life for all men. Still young and unsure of himself, the Captain feels uneasy in his new command, just a fortnight old. He does not yet know himself. He knows neither the good nor the bad within his own soul.

The Captain's physical appearance must be similar to his double or he would not assure the reader so many times that anyone looking at the two of them would think he was seeing double.

He is twenty-seven years old and was educated at Conway. His features are regular, eyes light, no growth on his cheeks; he wears a small brown moustache. He has a square, smooth forehead and a well-shaped, round chin. Most of the time both men wear identical sleeping suits of a grey striped pattern. When looking at Leggatt, the Captain feels as though he is looking at his own reflection "in the depths of a somber and immense mirror."

Leggatt

His physical appearance is so like the Captain's that the two appear to be twins. Leggatt, quite different from the Captain, is a man of violence. He killed a fellow sailor out of annoyance and shows no signs of regret or remorse. He was under arrest onboard the *Sephora*, where he served as first mate up to the time of his crime.

He also attended school at Conway and won swimming honors there; his athletic background accounts for his endurance in the water. He had to swim over two miles to reach the dangling ladder that saved him.

Leggatt's account of his fight with the seaman and his description of the final clinch that choked the man, smack of conceit. He seems to feel a satisfaction at having killed a man "who had no right to live." The poor wretch's right to live seems to have depended on Leggatt's whim.

During the course of his narrative, Leggatt reveals his contempt for all his sailing mates. The skipper is a coward; the second mate is a "grey-headed old humbug"; and the steward is a "dogmatic . . . loafer" who hates Leggatt like poison. The man whom he killed was an "ill-conditioned snarling cur."

When Leggatt explains why, when he had a chance, he did not kill the skipper, *his reason is not that he had any feeling of pity or mercy,* but that he would have been overpowered and "chucked back."

Leggatt shares the Captain's cabin for several dangerous days. The Captain feeds him on "stewed chicken, paté de foie gras, asparagus, cooked oysters, sardines" and other "sham delicacies" out of tins, as well as some fine preserves, all hidden in the Captain's own locker. Hard bread can always be gotten, and the Captain allows Leggatt to drink his morning coffee.

The Captain risks his very life and the safety of his ship and crew for this worthless scoundrel who returns not even so much as a thank-you.

Yet, in spite of this revelation of Leggatt's unsavory character, every reader will identify with him, pity him, and wish him well. No one would be happy or satisfied to see him fail in his final attempt to strike out for a new destiny. The reason for this paradox is that Leggatt is everyone's "dark self." Even as the Captain cherishes Leggatt, so the reader cherishes him. Such is the magic of Conrad's genius for characterization.

The Chief Mate

The Captain calls him "Terrible Whiskers," "Frightful Whiskers," and "Terrific Whiskers." Of a painstaking turn of mind, his dominant trait is to take everything under earnest consideration. "Bless my soul—you don't say so!" is his favorite saying.

The chief mate has found a scorpion in his cabin, and an analysis of the scorpion's reasons for "choosing his cabin" and "drowning himself" in his inkwell occupies him indefinitely.

The Second Mate

A round-cheeked, silent young fellow, grave beyond his years, he is the only man onboard younger than the Captain. He maintains a slightly scornful attitude toward the Captain.

The Steward

He seems to be an efficient chap who incurs the Captain's hatred because he innocently presents the greatest danger of discovery.

The *Sephora*'s Skipper

He has a face wreathed in thin red whiskers with "smeary" blue eyes. He is bandy-legged, and a spiritless tenacity appears to be his dominant quality. He mumbles his name "as though ashamed of it," but the Captain thinks that his name is Archbold. His only contribution to the plot is his description of Leggatt, whom he has always disliked, his few words about the man Leggatt killed, and his intention of reporting Leggatt dead by suicide.

Crewmen aboard the Ship

These men do not come into the story's foreground. They figure in the final climax under the overhanging menace of Koh-ring and the subsequent delight when the Captain skillfully brings his vessel around.

BRIEF PLOT SYNOPSIS

A nameless ship lies anchored in the Gulf of Siam. Her young Captain, also nameless, knows that his crew is tired from the loading operations they have just finished. In order to give them a good night's rest, he offers to omit the anchor watch and stay on deck himself until after midnight.

The Captain has been in command only a fortnight and feels that his crew still does not fully accept him. His feeling of alienation bothers him.

Before the crew turns in, the Captain sights another vessel about two miles distant. His second mate says the ship is the *Sephora*, loaded with coal, a hundred and twenty-three days out of Cardiff.

Later in the evening, his crew asleep, the Captain discovers that the ship's rope ladder still hangs over the side. He tries to pull it in and discovers that a naked man is hanging to it.

The man introduces himself as Leggatt and confesses that he escaped from the *Sephora*. He murdered a man several weeks ago and suffered confinement thereafter, but he managed to escape the *Sephora* and swim to the ship of the young Captain.

Even before the Captain brings out a pair of his own pajamas and makes his secret guest comfortable, he feels a strange identity with him. This feeling that Leggatt is his other self persists and increases. He hides the murderer in his own cabin at a fearful risk of discovery, and when the *Sephora's* skipper comes to search the Captain's ship for the escaped criminal, the Captain exerts fantastic efforts to protect the man.

After a few days, during which his feeling of duality with Leggatt mounts to near-madness, the Captain decides to allow his guest – his "secret sharer" – to escape at Koh-ring, an island headland where it will be possible to thrust his ship in close enough to shore for a swimmer to reach land.

His crew thinks he is mad and that he is taking the vessel to certain destruction. The Captain, however, handles his ship with such skill that he accomplishes his purpose of delivering his "secret sharer" and, at the same time, he elevates himself in the respect of his crew to the position he should occupy.

Both men strike out toward new destinies.

SUMMARIES AND COMMENTARIES

SECTION 1

Summary

Anchored at the mouth of the River Meinam in the Gulf of Siam, a sailing ship floats "in an immense stillness." Her young captain scans the calm sea and sees a cluster of rocky islets to his left. On his right, two clumps of trees mark the river's mouth and puffs of smoke show the path of the tug that has piloted his vessel down the river. He watches the tug disappear behind the great Paknam pagoda on its high green hill. The Captain reflects that the vessel seems to rest here at anchor in preparation for the long journey home to England. Nothing – not a bird, a canoe, or a cloud – moves in the whole tranquil scene.

In the changing light of the sunset, the Captain looks again toward the cluster of islands and sees something that ends his sense of solitude and cuts off his moment of communion with his ship. A "tide of darkness" flows over the scene.

Onboard, noises begin. The crewmen move about. The Captain finds his two officers awaiting him at the supper table in the lighted cuddy. He asks the chief mate if he has observed a ship's masts just beyond the high ridge of the largest island on their left.

The mate, distinguished by a "terrible growth of whiskers," makes his usual comment, "Bless my soul, sir! You don't say so!"

The second mate, young, round-cheeked, and quieter than most young men, smiles in a sneering way which annoys the Captain and reminds the Captain of *his* recent appointment as captain of the ship. He has been in charge of her only a fortnight, and he is (except for the second mate) the youngest man onboard. The other officers and crew have been together for eighteen months and feel familiar with one another. He alone is a newcomer; he even feels that he is a stranger to himself.

The whiskered chief mate speculates about the vessel which is anchored among the islands. Then the second mate comes up with full information which he acquired from the master of the river-tug. The ship is the *Sephora* out of Liverpool, has a cargo of coal, and is "a hundred and twenty-three days out of Cardiff." Both the Captain and the chief mate are annoyed by the second mate's cockiness.

The Captain knows that long days of loading cargo have tired his crew, and a generous impulse prompts him to order the crew to bed while he keeps the anchor watch the first half of the night. He sees that his unconventional order increases the suspicious curiosity with which the officers and men already regard him. The observation troubles him.

After the decks are cleared, he paces up and down contemplating his ship and finds her a fine vessel – roomy, clean, and inviting. He looks forward to his passage through the Malay archipelago, down the Indian Ocean, and up the Atlantic. He knows the route; only the vessel and her crew are unfamiliar. He comforts himself with the thought that his crew is like other crews, his ship like other ships, and even the sea is unlikely to surprise him with any unusual behavior.

Now the Captain discovers that the rope ladder, which had been put over for the master of the tug, still dangles on the vessel's side. He tries to haul it aboard, but a vigorous pulling jerks his body; the light ladder should haul in easily. Astonished, he looks over the ship's rail.

At once the Captain sees something attached to the ladder. It appears to be a headless, naked corpse. So astonished is he that the cigar he is smoking drops from his gaping mouth and lands with a hiss right beside the pale and headless wonder. At the hiss, the man's head appears. He lifts his face, and the Captain asks, "What's the matter?"

The man answers that he has cramps and adds that it is unnecessary to call anyone. The Captain says that he is master of the ship, and the mysterious swimmer introduces himself: "My name's Leggatt." He admits that he has been in the water since about nine o'clock the previous evening.

Leggatt asks if he can come aboard or if he will have to keep on swimming until he sinks from exhaustion. The Captain sees that these words are "no desperate formula of speech." The young swimmer actually considers such an alternative. Immediately a strong bond of unity is established between the two men.

Leggatt climbs the ladder while the Captain hurries to his stateroom and brings him a gray sleeping suit which is identical to the one he is wearing. Leggatt pulls on the sleepers, and the two men, dressed alike, confront each other. The Captain lifts a lighted lamp from the binnacle and studies the stranger's face. The sleeping suit fits him perfectly. He has a serious face with a concentrated and meditative expression and is probably about twenty-five years old.

"What is it?" the Captain asks Leggatt.

"An ugly business."

Leggatt tells the Captain that he was first mate on the *Sephora* and that he killed a man a few weeks before, during a violent storm. The Captain is the one who actually identifies the ship by name in the story—"Yes, I know. The *Sephora.*"

As the Captain looks upon his double in an identical sleeping suit, he has the uncanny feeling of facing his own reflection "in the depths of a somber and immense mirror."

Leggatt begins to defend his murderous action and describes his victim as a good-for-nothing wretch, "an ill-conditioned snarling cur."

The Captain identifies himself so intensely with the mysterious stranger that he is sure Leggatt can be no ordinary murderer. As Leggatt tells his story, the Captain does not need to ask for details, for he sees it happening "as though he were actually inside the other sleeping suit."

During Leggatt's narration of his crime, we learn that the murder occurred during a frightful storm. Leggatt explains how he and the other man were setting a reefed foresail at dusk when the man "gave me some of his cursed insolence." Leggatt felled him like an ox. The man jerked to his feet, and the two closed in furious struggle just as a tremendous wave rolled toward the ship. The two combatants did not see the danger. Leggatt had taken his victim by the throat when the weight of the water slammed them to the deck and washed them both unconscious, behind the fore-bits. For several minutes, the ship wallowed under a wash of water and foam. Later, when Leggatt regained consciousness, he found that he had been pried loose from his dead victim, that he had been relieved of his office as first mate, and that he had been locked up.

During the first part of Leggatt's story, the two men have been standing on the deck. Neither one has moved. It occurs to the Captain that should old "Whiskers" stick his head up the companionway, he would see some marvelous witchcraft—two identical Captains dressed in gray sleeping suits. Eager to avoid such an intrusion, the Captain hurries his double to his own stateroom.

A description of the Captain's "L"-shaped cabin follows. The small quarters must serve as shelter and refuge for the strange visitor as well as living space for the Captain.

In the strong light from the bulkhead lamp in the Captain's stateroom, Leggatt appears pale because of his weeks of confinement. Although the Captain realizes that Leggatt is really not at all like himself, the sense of duality persists and mounts.

Leggatt, in the security of the cabin, takes up his story again and relates how he escaped from the *Sephora* last evening at suppertime. He discovered that the steward had not locked his door. He strolled out on the quarter-deck and leaped into the ocean. He swam to one of the small islands where he took off his clothes, "tied them up in a bundle with a stone inside," and dropped them into the sea. Then he set out for another of the islets and saw the riding-lights of the Captain's homebound ship. He fixed his eyes on the lights and swam for the ship. He says the water "was like glass. One might have been swimming in a confounded thousand-feet cistern . . ." Then he reached the ship's ladder.

The Captain finds his "secret sharer" apprehensive of every noise on deck, anxious over every footstep. The Captain closes the porthole; then he tells Leggatt a little about himself and confesses that he is almost as much a stranger onboard this ship as his guest. He also suggests that it would take very little to make him "a suspect person in the eyes of the ship's company."

Leggatt pays little attention. He mentions the ladder and the miracle of its being forgotten and left dangling overboard, and he says that he thinks the *Sephora*'s officers will show up in the morning. The Captain is a little surprised at this prospect, but promises Leggatt that "we shall see then."

The Captain boosts Leggatt up into his sleeping berth. So tired is the exhausted swimmer that he needs the lift the Captain gives him. The Captain contemplates his double lying there in his bed-place and knows that he looks exactly like himself. He thinks of pulling the curtains, but extreme weariness strikes him also. He sits down on the couch and tries to throw off the sensation of being in two places at once. By morning the feeling of duality has increased, and the Captain's behavior is so peculiar that his officers appear to suspect him of madness or drunkenness.

Feeling the need to assert himself, the Captain shouts "the first particular order" he has given aboard ship and takes care to look "every foremast man" in the face. At breakfast, he presides with such frigid dignity that the officers are glad to escape his presence.

The Captain then awakens his double and contrives elaborate precautions for concealing him from the officers and crew. The two sharers of the Captain's cabin do not talk; it is too dangerous. Late in the morning a sailor brings news that a ship's boat is approaching. The Captain sees Leggatt give a start, and he immediately gives orders to get the ladder over. Then he goes on deck.

Commentary

This section is largely exposition. The author lets us see the characters aboard the ship, describes the vessel, especially the "L"-shaped cabin, which symbolizes Leggatt, and locates the geographical setting of the story. He introduces himself and reveals his feelings about the crew, the ship, and himself. His act of excusing his tired crew from deck duty and taking the anchor watch himself reveals his compassionate nature. His impulsive generosity, his feelings of insecurity in his new command, and his enthusiastic optimism demonstrate his youth.

He gives us a glimpse of the mysterious ship anchored a short distance away. (The ship will figure in the story.) He shows the sea to be like a calm lake – utterly tranquil, deserted, tropical and therefore warm – an ideal setting for a swimmer.

The ship, officers, and crew are all nameless. Not even the Captain is named. Conrad felt, perhaps, that the nameless sailors on a nameless ship would best symbolize the universal theme of his tale. In a sense, the Captain is every man; the ship is every man's ship of life.

The story moves well, and Conrad's use of mood expressions such as "tide of darkness," "my strangeness," and "mysterious shades of night" encourage expectancy in our minds. We know something dangerous or sinister is about to happen. When the rope ladder does not respond to the Captain's tugging, we anticipate some startling development, and we are not disappointed.

With Leggatt's appearance, the plot of the story gets underway. The Captain already has problems – strangeness and insecurity in his new command and also a lack of knowledge about himself. To his innermost soul, he is a stranger.

Leggatt's arrival augments his problems. He feels such a strong identity with the naked stranger that even the man's admission that he has killed a man does not repel the Captain. He feels that Leggatt is his other self, his twin soul. Now the Captain confronts his "dark self," the evil half of his dual nature. Such confrontations are simultaneously dangerous and enlightening.

At this point, Conrad's theme appears: *every person has a dark self.* Knowing and accepting one's total duality brings control and self-assurance.

Throughout Leggatt's confession of a violent and brutal murder, the Captain's chief concern seems to be protection for the man. He is so drawn to the stranger that he sympathizes with him as fully as though he himself had been an accomplice in the crime. He makes no comments such as one might expect from a responsible captain of a ship under such circumstances. When Leggatt concludes his story, all the Captain says is, "So you swam for our light?" Even this inane remark is spoken in a whisper. Yet it seems to underline the Captain's response – a genuine pleasure in the murderer's escape.

The Captain's response to Leggatt's story shows how fully he identifies with the fugitive. Leggatt also tells about himself: the son of a parson in Norfolk, a pupil in Conway (the same school the Captain attended), and a trusted officer on the *Sephora.* He emerges as a person of quality. Even the reader tries to discover extenuating circumstances which may relieve the guilt of his crime. Had there been no storm, perhaps the men would not have fought. Had the water not knocked the two men unconscious, perhaps the affair would have ended differently. Maybe Leggatt never really meant to murder the man. At least Leggatt did manage to set the reefed foresail which saved the ship. By such arguments the reader finds himself trying to justify the murder. Yet by Leggatt's own testimony, he hated the man and the man had "no business to live at all." He shows no sign of repentance but rather seems to gloat over the manner in which he killed his victim.

Through this section, the relationship with the secret guest develops until the Captain is like a man possessed. All his thoughts and efforts are directed to conceal and protect the murderer in his cabin. To the Captain, the man is not a bad person; he is so close that he seems his own self, his other self. Whenever he looks at him, it is with the tender regard that a man would bestow on his own hand or foot. Nothing escapes him – not a movement, not a sigh, not a look. The Captain is so fascinated that he has to glance at him every moment. And all the time he knows with a terrible certainty that this mysterious stranger from the sea is part of himself, a *sharer* of his soul. Every look he turns on Leggatt is a look at himself.

SECTION 2

Summary

The *Sephora's* skipper is not an imposing figure; red-haired, smeary-eyed, and bandy-legged, his outstanding characteristic is a "spiritless tenacity." The Captain, determined to protect his secret guest, decides to behave with extreme politeness. He thinks there is no other attitude which will thwart the *Sephora's* skipper. The Captain also feigns deafness in order that all the skipper's words will be spoken in so loud a voice that Leggatt, hiding in the stateroom, will surely hear and act accordingly.

The *Sephora's* skipper has come to hunt for his escaped mate. He relates the circumstances of the murder, the burial, Leggatt's escape, and details about the storm. Under the Captain's questioning, he admits that the foresail which Leggatt set saved the *Sephora,* but he is inclined to thank God rather than admit any obligation to the criminal. He seems taken aback by the Captain's calm politeness and perhaps also by the similarity between the Captain and his escaped mate. The Captain insists on showing him his own cabin and every cabin, locker room, and pantry – every single nook and cranny aboard the vessel. The *Sephora's* skipper still acts suspicious. He is "a tenacious beast," but says he will report Leggatt's disappearance as suicide and prepares to return to his ship. Even on the ladder, he lingers with another of his oblique queries. The Captain covers his question with a booming voice and bids him a final good-by.

After the skipper leaves, the members of the crew begin to discuss what they heard from the *Sephora's* boat crew who rowed the skipper over. They know the whole story now, and they are scandalized to think that anyone would even suspect this vessel of harboring a murderer.

The Captain feels it most trying to be on deck when his double is below in the stateroom; yet, being down there is trying too. However, he feels less torn apart when he is with his double. Now that Leggatt's story is known to all hands, it will be impossible to pass him off as anyone else. He dreads accidental discovery more now than at any time since the murderer came aboard.

Sunday comes and the quietness of the ship prevents any talk when the Captain goes down to his stateroom. The two sharers talk with their eyes. Later they whisper a little, and Leggatt describes more fully the *Sephora*'s ordeal during the violent storm, the skipper's panicked behavior, and his own bold action in setting the reefed foresail which saved the ship and the twenty-four men aboard.

A heavy knock clatters on the door, and a voice calls out that there is enough wind to get underway. The Captain goes out to meet the challenge of his first sailing experience with his new command. His sense of duality handicaps him so that he is unable to give any order spontaneously but must carefully think through each one. Even so, he finds himself whispering in the astonished mate's ear and moving with such stealth to look at the compass that the helmsman's eyes grow round with surprise. He knows that his crew and officers lean more and more to the idea that he is either a habitual drunkard or touched with madness.

There are scares, too, when discovery seems unavoidable. The Captain grows to hate the steward. He feels sure that the steward is the one who will certainly expose them. The fourth day out, the Captain's secret comes so near discovery that he admits, "My voice died in my throat and I went stony all over."

The cause of his terror is the trivial incident of the steward hanging a damp coat in the Captain's stateroom. The chance opening of the Captain's door could have disclosed the secret. The Captain is astonished that nothing so far has happened. He jumps to the conclusion that the secret sharer must have vanished. He finds Leggatt concealed in the narrow recessed part of the stateroom. Even Leggatt admits the narrowness of this escape. The Captain feels that he has "come creeping as near insanity as any man who has not actually gone over the border." He begins to wonder if Leggatt is not a figment of his imagination and invisible to all eyes but his own. Shouted orders on the deck break the spell, and the Captain marvels at Leggatt's composure. There is "something unyielding" in the man's character. He is not even agitated, yet his next words are, "It would never do for me to come to life again." A ghost might have spoken so. To every person but the Captain, Leggatt is a dead man.

Leggatt urges the Captain to let him off the ship among some islands off the Cambodian shore. The Captain at first pronounces the plan impossible. When Leggatt says he will go away in the Captain's sleeping suit and appeals to his perfect understanding, the Captain yields and admits that his objection has been sham sentiment, "a sort of cowardice." He agrees to let his visitor return to the sea the following night. There follows a short period of such deep communion between the two men that perfect understanding seems possible to them both. Leggatt admits, "It's very wonderful."

It is now midnight of the night when Leggatt must escape. The Captain, to the consternation of his officers and crew, sets the vessel on a tack that will bring her right in among the islands and reefs. He explains his irregular handling of the ship by saying that he is "hunting for the land breeze." The chief mate, at first critical, then concerned, then perplexed, becomes certain that the Captain is out of his mind.

The Captain now goes below to hold his last communion with his secret self. The two bend their heads over a map and decide that Leggatt's best chance lies on Koh-ring, a double-peaked island. The Captain is in his sleeping suit, as is Leggatt.

All day the vessel remains on its course, set to bring it right in under Koh-ring's towering mass. The crew members do not approve. They are terrified at the idea of running among the rocks and shoals by night, but the Captain refuses to alter his course by a single point. He orders the quarter-deck ports opened. When the second mate questions the order, the Captain cuts him off with sharp reproof.

Just before supper, the Captain, more restless than ever, goes down to give his "second self" final instructions regarding escape. Leggatt's lowering of himself into the water must be done quietly, and he must let himself down on a rope. The quarter-deck ports are open. Again there are mutual assurances of perfect understanding "from first to last."

For the first time, the Captain detects something faltering and strained in Leggatt's whispered words. Leggatt catches hold of the Captain's arm, but the supper bell breaks the intimate moment.

After supper, the Captain does not go below to his stateroom until after eight. As he opens his door, he has a back view of his "very own self" looking at a chart. The time has come to exchange their last whispers. They are fated never to hear each other's natural voices. The Captain opens a drawer, draws out three sovereigns, and urges them on Leggatt. He also provides a large silk handkerchief. Leggatt secures the handkerchief around his waist under his sleeper jacket. After a last long look into each other's eyes, the two shake hands and the Captain goes back on deck. He sees the hated steward puttering in the pantry, sends him off to the galley to get some hot water, and uses the moment of his absence to smuggle Leggatt into the sail locker. In a last gesture of protection, the Captain pulls off his big floppy hat and tries to jam it onto Leggatt's head. The man resists until he understands its purpose and then allows it. In the darkness, the men's hands grope for each other and "linger united in a steady, motionless clasp." They part in silence. When the steward returns, the Captain stands quietly by the pantry door.

Now the Captain feels it a matter of conscience to shave the shore as closely as he can. The enormous mass of Koh-ring's southern hill looms so close it seems one can reach out and touch it. He still holds to his course. The dark height seems to swallow the ship. The Captain calls for the mate and turns out all hands. The whole crew waits in agonized suspense upon the deck. The mate cries out, "Lost!" The Captain shuts him up and still insists that he is looking for the land wind. He finally gives the mate such a shaking that it jerks him out of his despair.

Then the Captain's command thunders through the ship, so that the watcher in the sail locker will not fail to hear. "Hard alee!" so close is the towering shadow of Koh-ring that his voice re-echoes as from a mountain gorge. Now is the moment. The secret stranger may already have dropped overboard.

The Captain is now able to forget Leggatt; he thinks only of his ship. Will he be able to bring her around? He sees that without some object to gauge his movement by, he cannot make it. Then he spots, on the smooth water, his own white hat, dropped by his "other self" as he struck out from the vessel's side. By means of the hat, the Captain brings the boat around to safety, while the crew exhibits every emotion of profound relief.

> Already the ship was drawing ahead. And I was alone with her. Nothing! No one in the world should stand now between us, throwing a shadow on the way of silent knowledge and mute affection, the perfect communion of a seaman with his first command.

The Captain looks back, and on the very edge of the darkness thrown by Koh-ring's towering mass, he catches a glimpse of his white hat marking the spot where his "other self" lowered himself into the water "to take his punishment: a free man, a proud swimmer striking out for a new destiny."

Commentary

The visit of the *Sephora's* skipper opens Section 2 of the story. By all the laws of the sea and the British Merchant Marine Service, the Captain should have delivered up his refugee to the proper authorities. Any revelation of such a scandal must certainly call down severe penalties. Yet the Captain does not even consider any course but concealment. He is committed as fully as though he were as much Leggatt as himself – as though his corporeal substance included both alike and on equal terms.

The Captain's method of confronting the skipper with haughty courtesy and feigned deafness is marked with such desperation and defiance as only the young – the hunted and hounded young – can know. And it works. The situation is saved.

The ship is now underway. The Captain has less time to spend with his second self; also there is more danger now. His sense of duality has grown now to the point where the Captain can hardly endure being separated from the physical presence of his twin soul. They are able to converse with their eyes, communication possible only to persons who are mysteriously close to one another. Note that the Captain hates the steward and other members of the crew who disturb his communion with his other self, or who threaten innocently to expose them. The thought of hating or blaming Leggatt never occurs to him. The idea of resenting all the trouble Leggatt has brought him does not enter the Captain's obsessed mind. He feeds Leggatt, nourishes, cherishes, shields him with infinite tenderness, and all Leggatt's danger has become the Captain's. He feels the sword hanging over his head too.

The soul union between the Captain and Leggatt deepens throughout this section. The sense of duality has now penetrated the Captain's mind almost to the point of instability. Note the emphasis placed upon the perfect understanding existing between them. Although the sense of duality is painful, understanding produces growth in the Captain. Although he objects to relinquishing his second self, his understanding has grown to the point where he can accept physical separation as the only means of preservation for his other self and therefore for his complete personality. He agrees to Leggatt's departure.

The Captain now issues the order that will make or break him. His whole future depends on successfully carrying out his desperate plan. His officers and crew are all but ready to mutiny. Yet so strong is his compulsion to deliver his secret self to anonymous safety that he does not hesitate to risk the vessel. Note that throughout this stressful day, the Captain is wearing his sleeping suit, straw slippers, and a floppy hat.

When the Captain goes down to give Leggatt final directions for his escape, the mysterious visitor shows the first signs of identification with the Captain that the Captain has felt for him.

Note too the closeness of the two men as they prepare to separate. Yet, as soon as the secret sharer is gone from the ship, the Captain immediately concentrates on the safety of his ship. He "hardly thought" of his other self. It seems that with his final assurance of Leggatt's successful deliverance, he draws himself into a complete person once more and is now a whole man, a forceful one, able to manage his ship and to command the respect of both officers and crew. The dangerous revelation is past. The Captain has faced and accepted his "dark self." Henceforth, he will be complete.

Note also how the final salvation for the Captain, ship, and crew hangs on the white hat, "the expression of my sudden pity for his mere flesh."

Conrad always chooses his closing words with care. It is not only Leggatt who is now "a free man, a proud swimmer striking out for a new destiny." The Captain is doing the same thing. Conrad's phrase "a new destiny" signifies the depths and heights of knowledge and experience never attainable until a man confronts and accepts his "dark self."

CRITICAL ESSAYS

HEART OF DARKNESS & *THE SECRET SHARER:* A COMPARISON

Conrad wrote these two works about the encounter with one's "dark self." The first one he wrote in 1899 – *Heart of Darkness,* a subtle and profound exploration of the subject through recounting his own adventures in the Congo. Conrad hid his meanings and challenged his readers to find them. Some readers did find rich treasure in the book, but many others seemed unable to grasp the deep significance of what Conrad intended to communicate.

One suspects that after ten years Conrad heard enough comment about his *Heart of Darkness* to realize that in order to reach the common mind with his important message, he must present it in a less subtle manner. Perhaps this is the reason why he wrote a much simpler story which bears essentially the same message.

In both stories the hero discovers a wicked person for whom he develops an irresistible attraction. In *Heart of Darkness*, Marlow is so eager to see and talk with Kurtz that he panics when he thinks he will never reach his goal. In *The Secret Sharer*, the Captain is so drawn to the murderer, Leggatt, that his mind all but gives way under the strain of obsession for his "dark self." In both stories the hero, who is a good person, identifies so fully with evil in the person of a murderer, that the two men almost become one, at least to the hero; thus they personify the potential for evil which co-exists in every man along with a potential for good.

Both stories happen in connection with a ship voyage. The ship signifies the ship of life, and any man's voyage through life may meet such adventures of the spirit.

Both stories end with deliverance for the hero. *Heart of Darkness* depicts a "dark self" (Kurtz) who dies as a god-like hero to the natives. *The Secret Sharer* shows Leggatt, who symbolizes the Captain's black soul, as he swims ashore at Koh-ring, delivered from death to seek a new destiny.

In both stories the white soul undergoes terrible suffering and danger in the final disposition of its black soul. Marlow looks into the abyss in his struggle with Kurtz in the forest just three hundred yards from the pagan convocation which hungers to adore Kurtz as a god. The Captain suffers his final conflict as he thrusts his ship closer and closer to the overhanging rock of Koh-ring, risking violent death for himself and his crew.

Through pity and kindness, Marlow subdues Kurtz and carries him back to his couch. Guided by the symbol of his pity (the white hat) for the erring humanity of his "dark self," the Captain releases his secret guest and swings his vessel back into safe channels.

SYMBOLISM

The entirety of *The Secret Sharer* is symbolic. The Captain symbolizes every man. The ship symbolizes every man's ship of life. The murderer, Leggatt, symbolizes every man's "dark self."

The Naked Swimmer

As Leggatt clings to the bottom rung of the ship's ladder, a number of symbols cluster around him. He is naked, stripped to his basic substance. Light seems to emanate from him, and later, phosphorescence glows about him. (Such light comes from decaying matter.) His color is *pale,* and he is immersed in "a greenish *cadaverous* glow." He appears to be a *"headless corpse."* The "sea lightning" plays about his limbs and gives him a *"ghastly"* look.

Familiarity with Conrad's use of symbols and mood-setting words indicates that what the Captain has found at the bottom of the ladder is nothing good, but the presence of light portends a possibility of good evolving from the circumstance.

The Scorpion

The whiskery chief mate finds a scorpion in his cabin, and the noxious creature causes him no end of speculation as to why it should have chosen *his* cabin and drowned itself in *his* inkwell. Certainly the *scorpion* in the mate's cabin and *Leggatt* in the Captain's cabin are of the same quality. Both are dangerous.

The scorpion's death by drowning in an inkwell may refer to Conrad himself, who seems to have drowned his own "dark soul" in a similar receptacle.

The White Hat

A symbol of good – specifically the Captain's pity for his "dark self" 's flesh. The white hat literally points the way to the Captain's success in bringing his ship around, thus insuring his acceptance and the salvation not only of himself but also that of his vessel and the lives of all who sail with him. The implication is that we should have pity on our "dark souls," forgive ourselves, and accept the duality within ourselves.

The Sleeping Suits

They symbolize the subconscious, where all communication between the "light soul" and the "dark soul" occurs. The suits are *gray,* further emphasizing the gray area where subconscious and conscious meet. The constant whispering between the Captain and his other self — the secret sharer — underlines the same half-dream quality of the adventure.

THEMES

Some of the themes in *The Secret Sharer* are
- Confrontation with one's dark self is both dangerous and enlightening.
- Every human soul has a "secret sharer," the dark companion of his better self.
- Pity and understanding for one's dark self are as important as acceptance of one's light self.
- Understanding and accepting one's duality of nature make soul-progress possible.

The compulsion to identify with both the Captain and the secret sharer is so great that many readers fail to recognize the evil nature of Leggatt. The scorpion symbol and the mood words that cluster about Leggatt's first appearance at the foot of the ship's ladder prove that Conrad regards the secret sharer as a wicked and dangerous character. Even the Captain, frightened into panic when the steward hangs a wet coat in his cabin, knows who will kill whom should the steward discover the intruder.

SUGGESTED ESSAY TOPICS

1. Why doesn't Conrad name any of the characters on the ship where the story happens?

2. What does the scorpion symbol suggest about the nature of the Captain's secret visitor?

3. Why might Conrad be interested in the dark side of people's souls?

4. What circumstances make the Captain's hiding of Leggatt in his cabin so dangerous?

5. Does Leggatt's account of the murder cause him to appear to be a good person who accidentally does wrong, or to be a bad person who intentionally and habitually does wrong?

6. Given the circumstances that surrounded Leggatt, would the Captain have committed murder?

7. Is knowledge of one's "dark self" beneficial or harmful?

8. Does the Captain find his compulsive attachment to Leggatt comforting or tormenting? Why?

9. Explain the Captain's new confidence after he has freed Leggatt at Koh-ring and swung his ship back into a safe channel.

10. Why does the reader want things to turn out well for Leggatt?

SELECTED BIBLIOGRAPHY

ALLEN, JERRY. *The Thunder and the Sunshine: A Biography of Joseph Conrad.* New York: Putnam, 1958.

BAINES, JOCELYN. *Joseph Conrad: A Critical Biography.* New York: McGraw-Hill, 1960.

BOYLE, TED E. *Symbol and Meaning in the Fiction of Joseph Conrad.* The Hague: Martinus Nijhoff, 1964.

CARROLL, WESLEY. "The Novelist as Artist," *Modern Fiction Studies,* I (February 1955), 2–8.

FORSTER, E. M. "Joseph Conrad: A Note," in *Abinger Harvest.* New York: Harcourt Brace, 1936.

GRAVER, LAWRENCE. *Conrad's Short Fiction.* Berkeley: University of California Press, 1969.

GUERARD, ALBERT J. "Introduction" to *Heart of Darkness* and *The Secret Sharer*. New York: Signet Books, 1950.

GURKO, LEO. *Joseph Conrad: Giant in Exile*. New York: Macmillan, 1962.

KRIEGER, MURRAY. "Joseph Conrad: Action, Inaction, and Extremity," in *The Tragic Vision: Variations on a Theme in Literary Interpretation*. New York: Holt, Rinehart and Winston, 1960.

MUDRICK, MARVIN, ed. *Conrad: A Collection of Critical Essays*. Englewood Cliffs, New Jersey: Prentice-Hall, 1966.

WRIGHT, WALTER F. *Romance and Tragedy in Joseph Conrad*. Lincoln: University of Nebraska Press, 1949.

ZABEL, MORTON DAUWEN. "Editor's Introduction" to *The Portable Conrad*. New York: Viking Press, 1947.

Get the Cliffs Edge

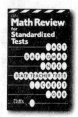

Advanced Placement Demands Advanced Preparation

Cliffs Advanced Placement® study guides are designed to give students that extra edge in doing their best on these important exams. The guides are complete, concise and focused providing you with all the information you need to do your best. Study with Cliffs Advanced Placement study guides for the kind of score that will earn you college credit or advanced standing.

- Thoroughly researched strategies, techniques and information
- Analysis of multiple-choice and essay questions
- Written by testing experts

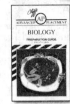

Legends In Their Own Time

Ancient civilization is rich with the acts of legendary figures and events. Here are three classic reference books that will help you understand the legends, myths and facts surrounding the dawn of civilization.

Cliffs Notes on Greek Classics and *Cliffs Notes on Roman Classics*—Guides to the idealogy, philosophy and literary influence of ancient civilization.

Cliffs Notes on Mythology—An introduction to the study of various civilizations as they are revealed in myths and legends.

Find these legendary books at your bookstore or order them using the form below.